A
JESUS-
SHAPED
LIFE

Cyrilia
Pratt

▼

A JESUS-SHAPED LIFE

Forty
Days
Toward
Christ-
likeness

STEVE CORDLE

 Seedbed

Printed in the United States of America

Cover design by Grace Boto at Terra Firma Studio
Page design and layout by PerfecType, Nashville, Tennessee

Cordle, Steve.
  A Jesus-shaped life : forty days toward Christ-likeness / Steve Cordle. –
Franklin, Tennessee : Seedbed Publishing, ©2021.

    pages ; cm .

    ISBN 9781628249224 (paperback)
    ISBN 9781628249231 (Mobi)
    ISBN 9781628249248 (ePub)
    ISBN 9781628249255 (uPDF)
    OCLC 1273731459

    1. Jesus Christ--Example--Prayers and devotions.   2. Jesus
    Christ—Character--Prayers and devotions.   3. Devotional
    calendars   I. Title.

BT304.2.C57 2021   232   2021948549

 Seedbed

SEEDBED PUBLISHING
Franklin, Tennessee
seedbed.com

For Logan, Hope, and Grayson:
I am cheering you on as you grow in Jesus.

Contents

Week 3
The Relationships of Jesus

Week 4
The Courage of Jesus

Week 5
The Justice of Jesus

Week 6
The Mission of Jesus

Introduction

"Whoa," whisper onlookers. Others gaze silently, awed by the startling beauty of what lies before them.

More than five million people visit the Grand Canyon every year, and no one seeing it for the first time can be adequately prepared for the stunning view. The depth, color, and scope are impossible to describe. Pictures cannot do it justice. One of the most spectacular geological sites in the world, the Grand Canyon extends up to 18 miles wide and six thousand feet deep. It stretches for 277 miles and contains several ecosystems.

Geologists tell us that the Colorado River carved the canyon over millions of years. The river cut so deep that its strata reveal 40 percent of the earth's history. Even today, the relentless water flow continues to imperceptibly erode the canyon floor, deepening and widening it.

Whether we realize it or not, there are seen and unseen forces working on our hearts and minds too. Our thinking, values, and character are continually being shaped by myriad influences. Some of them are obvious, such as our family of origin, nationality, or education. Our life experiences—both the painful and the enjoyable—also significantly shape us.

Other influences go unnoticed. Take, for example, our cell phones. Tony Reinke writes that heavy cell phone use leaves us continually distracted. As we check our phones an average of three hundred times per day, we ignore the people and events around us.[1] Similarly, our interaction with the Internet fragments our ability to focus and reduces our attention span.[2] Algorithms increasingly determine what we see and, thus, affect what we think.

If all that sounds disconcerting, here is some good news: if you are a follower of Jesus, there is also a supernatural force at work in your life shaping you in healthy, life-giving ways. That force is the power of God forming you into the image of Jesus.

Romans 8:28–29 says:

> And we know that in all things God works for the good of those who love him, who have been called according to his purpose. For those God foreknew he also predestined to be *conformed to the image of his Son*. (emphasis added)

God's eternal goal is that we live a Jesus-shaped life. From the moment you trusted Christ, God began the process of making you like his Son. And Philippians 2:12–13 urges us to engage in our part of that process: "Work out your own salvation with fear and trembling, for it is God who works in you to will and to act in order to fulfill his good purpose."

---

1. Tony Reinke, *12 Ways Your Phone Is Changing You* (Wheaton, IL: Crossway, 2017).
2. Mike Wright and Ellie Zolfagharifard, "Internet Is Giving Us Shorter Attention Spans and Worse Memories, Major Study Suggests," *Telegraph*, June 6, 2019, https://www.telegraph.co.uk /technology/2019/06/06/internet-giving-us-shorter-attention -spans-worse-memories-major/.

It is God's power that shapes us into the image of Jesus, but we are not passive. Unlike the rock in the Grand Canyon that lies motionless as it is molded by the river, we are actively engaged in a cooperative effort with God. Philippians 2 says that God works in us, and we work out our salvation. He acts, and we respond with the strength he provides. When it comes to becoming like Christ, without God we cannot, and without us, God will not. The Lord will not force us to become like Jesus against our will.

Notice the verse does not say we are to work *for* our salvation. Salvation is a gift of God's grace that we receive, not earn. We are to work *out* our salvation. We already received our salvation; now, we are to develop it.

It is similar to a physical workout. You don't work *for* your arms—they were given to you at birth. You work *out* your arms; that is, you exercise to strengthen them. Once we freely receive new life in Christ, we begin the process of becoming like him. As we work more of Jesus' life into our habits, routines, and character, we grow in his image.

About This Book

This book is designed to be read over a forty-day period, ideally as part of a small-group experience. Each week explores one aspect of Jesus' nature and what it looks like for us to share in it. The Working It Out section at the end of each week is a menu of spiritual exercises to help you to process and apply what you've read. Putting God's truth into practice is vital because hearing his Word without responding to it stagnates our growth and diminishes our sensitivity to the Holy Spirit. Conversely, applying what we hear results in growth and spiritual maturity.

At the same time, it is impossible to change our lives in forty different ways over forty days, so be selective. At the end of each week, ask yourself which reading stood out to you the most. Perhaps that is the Holy Spirit's arrow pointing you to the next area of growth he has for you.

Because spiritual growth happens best in community, small-group questions are included. They are designed to prompt you to share your journey with a few trusted friends. After all, we are transformed as we serve and are served, as we love and are loved. That is why the New Testament gives us forty-seven "one another" commands, such as "Love one another" (John 15:12 NASB) and "Bear one another's burdens" (Gal. 6:2 NASB). Our spiritual journey is personal but not private. So, read the daily reflections, and gather weekly with others who are on the journey to pray and encourage one another in your action steps.

Of course, becoming like Jesus will take longer than forty days. But do not be discouraged; it will happen. Philippians 1:6 says, "Being confident of this, that he who began a good work in you will carry it on to completion until the day of Christ Jesus."

And on that day, when Christ's work in you is completed, you will reflect the image of Jesus to such a degree that onlookers may whisper, "Whoa."

A
JESUS-
SHAPED
LIFE

Week 1

Made for This

God's will is for you to be holy . . .
> —1 Thessalonians 4:3 NLT

For those God foreknew he also predestined to be conformed to the image of his Son, that he might be the firstborn among many brothers and sisters.
> —Romans 8:29

Who are you going to live for—yourself or God?
> —Rick Warren

Day 1

Desiring What
God Desires

▶ **Read Ephesians 1:1–4.**

Even before Todd was born, his father had plans for him. Marv would make Todd the perfect quarterback.

Football ran in the family. Marv had been a captain for the University of Southern California and played professionally. Todd's uncle had been a star quarterback at USC. Now that Marv had a son, he intended to raise Todd to surpass them both.

Marv gave Todd frozen kidney to teethe on as an infant. Marv was stretching Todd's hamstrings when Todd was one month old, and had him doing push-ups before he could walk. Todd's parents made sure that he adhered to the purest diet: no junk food and no sugar. Todd even brought his own cake to birthday parties. *Sports Illustrated* later called Todd "America's first test-tube athlete" and reported that he had never eaten a Big Mac or an Oreo.

For a while, it seemed that the plan was working. Todd excelled as a quarterback in high school and went on to play at USC. After college, the Oakland Raiders drafted him in the first round.

But all was not as it seemed.

Todd always wanted to please his overbearing father, but he also wanted to be a normal kid. In grade school, Todd started sneaking junk food, and by high school, he was smoking marijuana regularly.[1] In college, he broke free from the strict rules of his upbringing. He began a struggle with harder drugs that shortened his professional career and plagued him for the rest of his life.

Eventually, the pressure became too much for Todd. During his freshman year at USC, he briefly left school and confessed to his mother, "I wish I could go somewhere else and be someone else. I don't want to be Todd Marinovich."[2] In short, Todd did not want to be the man his father desired him to become.

Have you ever felt that way in your relationship with God? While wanting to please your heavenly Father, have you wondered whether you can measure up to his expectations? Perhaps you're not always sure you want to, even if you feel you should.

Our image of what God desires of us determines how we relate to him. If we believe that God wants us to live in a way that we consider unappealing, we will keep our distance from him. So, if we want a trust-filled relationship with God, we need to desire what he wants for us.

---

1. Michael Rosenberg, "Learning to be Human Again," *Sports Illustrated*, January 11, 2019, https://www.si.com/nfl/2019/01/11/todd-marinovich-dad-marv-quarterback-drugs-rehab.

2. Douglas S. Looney, "The Minefield," *Sports Illustrated*, September 3, 1990.

And what is it that God desires for us? It might not be what we think it is.

Ephesians 1:4 tells us: "Even before he made the world, God loved us and chose us in Christ to be holy and without fault in his eyes" (NLT).

God wants to make us holy. Does that idea inspire you or induce you to cringe? Your answer likely depends on what you believe it means to be holy. If you think that *holy* is a code word for well-behaved, you probably won't be enthusiastic about it. If you imagine holiness to be a grim, duty-bound existence, you might say, "I'll pass." But, in reality, true holiness bears no resemblance to those tired stereotypes.

Holy is the word the Bible uses to describe God's character. Holiness is not sterile rule-keeping; it is the word that sums up God's goodness and his power.[3] Holiness is wholeness. It is our interior and exterior life syncing up with heaven's heartbeat. It shows up as life-giving words, thoughts, and actions. Holiness is life as God originally intended it to be. In short, to be holy means to be like Jesus. And God created us for that life.

"Even before he made the world, *God loved us.*" God wants us to be like Jesus because he loves us, not because it annoys him if we are not. He knows how rich and rewarding it is to live a Jesus-shaped life, and he desires that for us.

God desires to free us from both the penalty and the power of sin. We can be eternally grateful that God forgives us and promises us heaven after we die. Yet, he also makes it possible for us to taste the kingdom of

---

3. "Holiness," *The Bible Project*, accessed August 31, 2019, https://thebibleproject.com/explore/holiness/.

heaven here and now. God loves us too much to leave us trapped in the grip of sin that robs us of peace, tears apart our relationships, and blocks us from fulfilling his plan for our lives. While it is wonderful to know that we are forgiven for our disobedience, it is exhilarating to be liberated from the compulsion to repeat that sin.

Do we want a Jesus-shaped life? Do we desire what God wants for us? When we see the fulfilling life God has in mind for us, will we desire it? Admittedly, as we grow there will be moments (maybe seasons) when we want our own way. Saint Augustine once prayed, "Lord, make me chaste [sexually pure], but not yet!"[4] But the good news is that if we ask him, the Holy Spirit will change our desires to match God's good ones for us.

Take a moment now to talk with God about your feelings regarding a Jesus-shaped life. Be honest with him. Where do you want his will? Where have you not yet embraced it?

▶ Prayer

Lord, thank you for your love for me. I know you want the best for me. By your Spirit, help me to want what you want for me. Amen.

---

4. Saint Augustine, *Confessions*, trans. Henry Chadwick (New York: Oxford University Press, 1991), 145.

Day 2

Why Christlikeness Is Not Natural

▶ **Read Ephesians 4:22–24.**

The movie *The Lord of the Rings: The Two Towers* features a grotesque character named Gollum. Before he came to possess the "one ring to rule them all," he used to be a hobbit named Sméagol. But, gradually, the power of the ring distorted his body and mind, turning the wholesome hobbit into the ghastly Gollum.

Eventually, Gollum loses the ring, and a hobbit named Frodo acquires it. Gollum pursues Frodo, scheming to regain possession of the ring by any means necessary. Yet when Frodo meets Gollum, he doesn't harm the creature. Instead, he reminds him of his prior life and name. As a result, Gollum begins to call Frodo, "Master," and becomes an uneasy ally in his quest.

Later, however, Gollum's old, twisted nature resurfaces. One night, as Sam and Frodo sleep, Gollum is tempted to steal the ring. However, he is torn. One part of him wants to betray Frodo, but another part of him doesn't. His old Gollum nature wants to take the ring. But his new Sméagol nature wants to help Frodo. The two natures argue with one another:

> Gollum: "We wants it. We needs it. Must have the Precious. They stole it from us. Sneaky little hobbitses. Wicked. Tricksy. False."
>
> Sméagol: *(shaking his head)* "No. Not Master."
>
> Gollum: *(snarling malevolently)* "Yes . . . They will cheat you, hurt you, lie!"
>
> Sméagol: "Master's my friend."
>
> Gollum: "You don't have any friends. Nobody likes you."
>
> Sméagol: *(closes his ears with is hands)* "Not listening. I'm not listening."
>
> Gollum: "You're a liar and a thief."
>
> Sméagol: "No."
>
> Gollum: (sinister whisper) "Murderer!"
>
> Sméagol: (voice breaking; hurt by Gollum's remark) "Go away!"[5]

Most of us know what it's like to argue with ourselves—to engage in an internal struggle. If you have ever tried to lose weight, you may have had a conversation that goes something like this:

> New healthy self: "I'm not going to eat that donut!"
>
> Old undisciplined self: "Yes, you are. You know you are. Just admit it."
>
> New healthy self: "No, I'm not! I eat healthy now!"

---

5. Concept from Preaching Today, https://www.preachingtoday .com/search/?query=Gollum&sourcename=Illustrations &order=newest&type=.

Old undisciplined self: "You'll never really change. You know it's just a matter of time until you cave in. You may as well do it now and enjoy it."

If improving our eating habits is difficult, how much more challenging is it to change our very character from self-oriented to Christlike? Toning up our bodies is difficult; how much harder is it to grow into the image of Jesus?

Anyone who has followed Jesus for more than a couple of weeks knows that becoming Christlike can be a struggle at times. We can honor Jesus one minute, only to stumble into sin the next.

The reason we wrestle with those inner battles is that we have two natures. Ephesians 4:22–24 tells us we have an "old self" and a "new self."

You were taught, with regard to your former way of life, to put off your *old self*, which is being corrupted by its deceitful desires; to be made new in the attitude of your minds; and to put on the *new self*, created to be like God in true righteousness and holiness. (emphasis added)

The old self is the nature with which we were born. It is our human nature, and it is not like Jesus. Verse 22 says it is being corrupted. It does not want what God wants.

Our new self, however, comes from God. The moment we put our faith and trust in Jesus, the Holy Spirit creates a new spirit in us. This new nature is made in the likeness of God. Our new self desires holiness. It is comfortable with Christlikeness.

Ephesians 4 tells us how to respond to each of our two natures. We're told to "put off" the old nature. We don't become like Jesus by struggling to reform our old nature. Life in Jesus is not about managing our sin. We become Christlike by receiving an entirely new nature.

Verse 24 tells us to "put on" the new self. Becoming like Jesus is the process of learning to respond to the new self and to ignore the old one. God doesn't ask us to improve our old nature; we are exhorted to kill it—that is, to consider it dead by ignoring it. We are to refuse to give it what it demands.

However, the old nature doesn't leave quietly. When the New Gollum (Sméagol) told the Old Gollum to go away, the Old Gollum mockingly asked: "Go away?"

> Sméagol: "I hate you. I hate you."
>
> Gollum: "Where would you be without me? . . .
>   I saved us. It was me. We survived because
>   of me."
>
> Sméagol: "Not anymore."
>
> Gollum: "What did you say?"
>
> Sméagol: "Master looks after us now. We don't
>   need you."
>
> Gollum: (appalled) "What?"
>
> Sméagol : "Leave now, and never come back!"

As the New Gollum realizes there's no counter-response, he jumps and rejoices: "Gone! Gone! We told him to go away, and away he goes! Gone, gone, gone! Sméagol's free!"

Do not be discouraged in your wrestling with your old self. Remember that you have a new nature that comes from God. You do not need to take orders from your old one. As you learn to ignore it, you will find that it will back down and weaken. You, too, will say, "I told him to go away, and away he goes! I'm free!"

▶ Prayer

Lord Jesus, thank you for the new nature you have given me. Help me to ignore my old self and live by the power of your Holy Spirit. Amen.

Day 3

Is Change Even Possible?

▶ Read Romans 6:1–4.

"Mom, I want to play football."

I was thirteen years old and feeling inspired by the NFL game I was watching on TV. Although I often played football in the backyard with my friends, I wanted to try out for an organized team.

My mother wisely replied, "Baseball season will be here soon." I was a skinny kid with little upper body strength, and she did not have the heart to tell me I wasn't cut out to be a football star. I tried eating more and working out, but eventually, I had to concede—I did not have a future in football.

Each of us confronts our limitations at some point. Whether our goal is to perform a screaming guitar solo or to earn an A in organic chemistry, sometimes, despite our best efforts, our dreams never become reality.

Is a Jesus-shaped life one of those unrealistic pipe dreams? Is holiness an unattainable goal that God expects us to work toward, all the while knowing that we'll never reach it? No one likes to fight a losing battle. If we can't change, we might as well accept defeat and content ourselves with appreciating God's forgiveness when we fail.

Some Christians do just that. Maybe you've seen the bumper sticker that reads: "Christians aren't perfect, just forgiven." That is true as far as it goes, but it doesn't go far enough. That saying implies that the only difference between Christ-followers and everyone else is that God forgives us and not them.

However, Jesus tells us something different. In Matthew 5:13–14, he says, "You are the salt of the earth. . . . You are the light of the world." We can't be salt and light if we live the same way the world does. Jesus expects us to stand out from our culture.

God's forgiveness is an amazing gift, but he wants to do more than take away our guilt. First John 1:9 promises: "If we confess our sins, he is faithful and just *and will forgive us our sins and purify us from all unrighteousness*" (emphasis added).

God promises to both forgive us *and* change us. He will purify us so that we do not have to keep falling into the same sins. Jesus said, "Very truly I tell you, everyone who sins is a slave to sin. . . . So if the Son sets you free, you will be free indeed" (John 8:34, 36).

We are not just sinners saved by grace. We are also children of God set free from sin by Jesus. Romans 6:1–2 asks: "What shall we say, then? Shall we go on sinning so that grace may increase? By no means! We are those who have died to sin; how can we live in it any longer?"

Theologians will debate exactly how much freedom from sin we can experience in this life, but here is what we need to know: *there is no sin from which Jesus cannot free us.*

Is there a habit or sin that has harassed you? Jesus can deliver you.

For example, if you have a habit of exploding in anger, you don't need to say, "Well, when I was growing up, my family screamed at each other. It's just how I am wired." That might be true. Perhaps responding in anger was your default setting. But that was the old you. The new nature God birthed in you is free to be patient. You do not need to be a slave to anger. The same is true for any other sin; you don't need to accept its control over you.

Ginger Whitacre had been praying for her husband, Mark, for ten years, and his parents had been praying for even longer. But Mark wasn't changing. He was gripped by materialism, status, and power. At age thirty-two, he was already a division president of one of the nation's largest companies. He had an extraordinary salary, lived in a mansion, and flew in his own corporate jet.

Even so, Mark was not content. He was driven by a constant, relentless craving for more. He became a workaholic and a stranger to his wife and kids. Eventually, his greed led him to participate in his company's billion-dollar price-fixing scheme.

One day, Ginger learned that Mark was breaking the law and forced him to go to the FBI to report it. The authorities gave him a choice: wear a wire to record his colleagues or go to jail. He chose to wear the wire. For three years, Mark secretly collaborated with the FBI to build a case against his employers. In the end, several executives went to jail, including Mark. Although he had complete immunity in the price-fixing case, he was so firmly in the grip of greed that he could not resist stealing millions of dollars from his company even while he was working with the FBI. It was illogical, but Mark was a slave to greed.

In spite of it all, Ginger kept praying for him. Finally, while he sat in jail, Mark became a follower of Jesus. He said, "I became a free man in prison." He was powerfully changed. He was liberated from the grip of greed. His whole perspective on life was transformed.

For the last thirteen years, Mark has lived a Jesus-shaped life. After his release, he took an entry-level job and later rose to become chief operating officer of the company, leading research efforts in cancer prevention and the global battle against HIV. Today, corporations invite him to speak about business ethics at their training events. He is also a leading spokesman for Christian Business Men's Connection. He said, "I am not looking for forgiveness. [He found that in Christ.] I am looking to show people who have fallen short, as I have, that there is an opportunity to turn one's life around."[6]

▶ Prayer

Lord, help me to expect change by your power so that I can see myself as a new creation in Christ. Amen.

---

6. Walter Pavlo, "A Presidential Pardon Long Overdue for Whistleblower Mark Whitacre," *Forbes*, May 31, 2018.

Day 4

Marked by Grace

▶ **Read Isaiah 6:1–7.**

Isaiah had been worshiping at the temple in Jerusalem for decades. He was familiar with the layout of the courts, the rhythm of the prayers, and the smell of the incense. He often stood silently, head bowed, outside the Holy of Holies, where God's presence dwelt.

One day Isaiah was jolted out of his routine by a surprise encounter with the living God:

> It was in the year King Uzziah died that I saw the Lord. He was sitting on a lofty throne, and the train of his robe filled the Temple. Attending him were mighty seraphim, each having six wings. With two wings they covered their faces, with two they covered their feet, and with two they flew. They were calling out to each other:
>
> "Holy, holy, holy is the Lord of Heaven's Armies!
>   The whole earth is filled with his glory!"

Their voices shook the Temple to its foundations,
and the entire building was filled with smoke.
(Isa. 6:1–4 NLT)

Ushered into the presence of God, Isaiah was utterly undone. He was staggered by the unfiltered sight of God's majesty and holiness. He glimpsed the God who is not just holy but "holy, holy, holy."

Isaiah didn't respond by saying, "Awesome! Wait 'til everybody sees this on Instagram!" No, when Isaiah encountered the holiness of God, he became aware of his unworthiness to be in God's presence.

Then I said, "It's all over! I am doomed, for I am
a sinful man. I have filthy lips, and I live among
a people with filthy lips. Yet I have seen the King,
the Lord of Heaven's Armies." (v. 5 NLT)

Isaiah was a respected religious and national leader. Some regarded him as a holy man. But when he came face-to-face with the holiness of the Lord, Isaiah realized that his sin and God's glory could not mix. He was sure he was doomed. But instead, Isaiah was surprised by grace.

Then one of the seraphim flew to me with a burning
coal he had taken from the altar with a pair of
tongs. He touched my lips with it and said, "See,
this coal has touched your lips. Now your guilt is
removed, and your sins are forgiven." (vv. 6–7 NLT)

Isaiah was literally touched by God's grace where he most needed it. His lips were a source of shame to him ("I have filthy lips"), and that is exactly where the angel applied the coal.

Isaiah's experience shows us four truths that shape us on our journey toward Christlikeness:

Truth #1: We need deep spiritual healing.

When Isaiah saw the Lord, he realized that there was a huge holiness gap between himself and God. It's not just that he said and did some wrong things; he recognized that his very being was out of sync with God's ("I am a sinful man"). If you or I caught a glimpse of the glorified Jesus right now, we would realize that, apart from him, we could not stand in his presence.

Truth #2: God accepts us by grace.

God saw Isaiah's sin but did not reject him. Isaiah didn't plead his case or make excuses for his sin. He admitted his moral neediness. The Lord forgave and purified him out of undeserved mercy, not because Isaiah promised to shape up or be a better person. Isaiah received mercy.

God sent Jesus as our atoning sacrifice. We are saved by grace through faith in him (Eph. 2:8–9). We don't pursue Christlikeness so that God will accept us. We seek a Jesus-shaped life because God has *already* accepted us. When we remain anchored to this truth, we will not sink into discouragement or anxiety.

Truth #3: God transforms us by grace.

We do not have what it takes to become like Jesus. No amount of self-control or good intention will transform us. But the good news is that we don't need to have what it takes—because God does! God's grace not only forgives us, it also transforms us.

Hang with me for just a couple of paragraphs of theology.

John Wesley taught about three types of grace: prevenient grace, justifying grace, and sanctifying grace. These are labels we use for the different ways God works in us. Let me explain why this matters to you.

First, you need to know that following Christ was not your idea; it was God's. Even before you wanted to be a Christ-follower, the Holy Spirit was drawing you toward Jesus. That work of the Spirit is called *prevenient grace*. You didn't deserve or ask for God to draw you to himself; he just did it.

Then, when you responded to the Spirit's tug by putting your faith in Jesus, God forgave you and made you right with himself (Rom. 5:1). That work of God is called *justifying grace*—it is the grace that saves us (Eph. 2:8–9).

And after you became a child of God through faith, God began to make you more like Jesus. This work is called *sanctifying grace*. It is what the apostle Paul wrote about in Philippians 1:6: "Being confident of this, that he who began a good work in you will carry it on to completion until the day of Christ Jesus."

By grace, God's Spirit drew you to himself. By grace, God forgave you and graciously gave you a new nature. Do you think he is going to quit working by grace now? Do you think he'll say, "I've taken you this far. It's up to you from here on. Good luck. See you in heaven . . . maybe"?

No, God does not leave us to our own devices. He is at work in you right now. He is the one who has given you the desire to be more like Jesus. He will also give you the power to do it. Yes, we have a part to play in this process. Spiritual transformation is a joint venture between God and us. We grow by cooperating with the Holy Spirit's work in us. (That is what you're doing right now by reading this book!)

Truth #4: Grace propels us toward mission.

Isaiah's story does not end with being forgiven by God's grace. After he was cleansed inwardly, he received a new focus for his life.

> Then I heard the Lord asking, "Whom should I send as a messenger to this people? Who will go for us?"
>
> I said, "Here I am. Send me." (Isa. 6:8 NLT)

Isaiah spent the rest of his life on a faith adventure that made an eternal impact. And you and I can too. As we let the Holy Spirit transform us more into the image of Jesus, a new purpose will open up for us. And it is all by grace.

▶ Prayer

Lord, thank you for your grace, which drew me to seek you, saved me, and is now transforming me into the image of Jesus. Amen.

$Day\ 5$

Our Ultimate Life Coach

▶ **Read John 16:5–15.**

I spent the summer after my freshman year in college coaching twelve-year-old boys at an overnight baseball camp. I instructed campers in the fundamentals of a compact swing, running the bases, and getting in front of ground balls. My favorite task, though, was coaching pitchers. I worked alongside the camp's owner, who had pitched professionally. We demonstrated wind-up, delivery, and follow-through techniques. Then we watched the kids as they threw. If we saw a camper shift his weight at the wrong time, we stopped him and reminded him of the proper form. If his lead foot came down in the wrong spot, we stepped in to correct it.

As coaches, the last thing we wanted to do was to discourage the kids by pointing out what they were doing wrong; our goal was quite the opposite. We were there to help them to become the best baseball players they could be. We corrected their pitching mechanics so they could throw strikes and get batters out. We looked for flaws in their swings so that they could eliminate them and drive the ball farther. We knew that improving their skills would help them enjoy the game more.

The job of a coach is to help players achieve new levels that they would not reach on their own. Sometimes that means that a coach will say, "Not that way; do it this way."

Even adults pay people to tell them what they should do differently. Nobody hires a piano teacher to tell them how lovely they play. No, they hire a teacher to instruct them on how to perform better. That means sometimes the teacher will stop the student and say, "That's not the right rhythm; it goes like this." People hire a personal trainer to help them improve their fitness. They expect the trainer to push them: "Don't quit now! Give me ten more reps!"

The Holy Spirit is our ultimate life coach. He knows that God created us to become like Jesus, and he will encourage and correct us toward that end.

Speaking about the Holy Spirit, Jesus told his disciples: "And He, when He comes, will convict the world regarding sin, and righteousness, and judgment" (John 16:8 NASB). Just like a good coach, the Holy Spirit will sometimes tell us, "Not that way; do it this way instead." That is called conviction.

The Spirit's conviction can take the form of a sudden realization or an inner catch. For example, if I walk away from a conversation and think, *I shouldn't have said that*, it is possible that the Holy Spirit is convicting me. He may be trying to tell me that Jesus would have spoken differently than I did. That can prompt me to apologize and to speak with a different tone in the future.

Conviction is not the Holy Spirit saying, "Gotcha!" His aim is not to scold us; it is to redirect us. The Holy Spirit wants to get our attention so that he can show us a better way—Jesus' way. He is alerting us of our need for change because he is for us.

A few years ago, I was worshiping with our congregation. Just before I stepped up to preach, one of our staff tapped me on the shoulder and whispered, "Your fly is open." I felt my face grow pale. I was mortified. I corrected the situation as quickly and discreetly as possible. Then, a second emotion filled me: gratitude. I was thankful that he told me *before* I stood in front of hundreds of people and not after! When I thanked him later, he replied: "Friends tell each other these kinds of things."

The Holy Spirit is our friend. Through conviction, he taps us on the shoulder to tell us when we need to change. He will convict us, but he will never condemn us. There is a big difference.

Conviction is specific. When we are convicted, we can name a particular action or attitude that God wants to change. For example, "I did not tell the truth to my boss," or, "I took what didn't belong to me." Conviction is not an enjoyable feeling, but the Spirit's purpose is not to shame us; it is to transform us.

By contrast, condemnation is general. Instead of saying, "You acted in an un-Christlike way," condemnation says, "You are a bad person."

Conviction corrects us. Condemnation accuses us. Conviction comes from God; condemnation comes from Satan. (In fact, the name *Satan* means "accuser," or "adversary.")

Romans 8:1 says, "Therefore, there is now no condemnation for those who are in Christ Jesus." When you put your faith in Jesus, you were completely forgiven. You became a child of God, and your heavenly Father loves you. He will lead you to maturity, not punish you or shame you. As you seek to be Christlike, be sure you are listening to the prompting of the Holy Spirit and not to the accusations of Satan.

We cannot become like Jesus by trusting our judgment alone. We need an outside perspective. Thankfully, the Lord has sent us the ultimate life coach: the Holy Spirit. He will convict us through a variety of means: other people, inner prompts, circumstances, Scripture, and more. And best of all, he will empower us to make the changes he prompts.

▶ Prayer

Holy Spirit, "Search me . . . and know my heart; test me and know my anxious thoughts. See if there is any offensive way in me, and lead me in the way everlasting" (Ps. 139:23–24). Amen.

Day 6

The First Word in Transformation

▶ **Read Matthew 4:12–17.**

A person's last words can be both fascinating and revealing. And so can their first. Writer George Orwell's first word as a baby was *beastly*. When he was around eighteen months old, he caught a severe case of bronchitis and was confined to bed. It was there he spoke that first word. Ironically, he used the word *beastly* in every book he wrote except for his novel about beasts, *Animal Farm*.

Pablo Picasso could draw before he could speak. He first learned to ask for things by drawing pictures of them. His first word was *piz*, which was the way he pronounced *lápiz*, the Spanish word for "pencil." The world is grateful that his mother gave him one.[7]

The book of Matthew records that the first word Jesus spoke in his public ministry was *repent*. In Matthew 4:17,

---

7. Arika Okrent, "First Words of 11 Famous People," October 11, 2013, http://mentalfloss.com/article/53129/first-words-11-famous -people.

Jesus announced: "Repent, for the kingdom of heaven has come near." He was declaring that a new way of life had arrived—the "kingdom of heaven" (or "the kingdom of God"). The kingdom of God can be defined as life when God is in charge. With his first words, Jesus told us to repent so that we could experience this new way of life God designed for us.

To live a new way, we need to stop following our old routines. That is what repentance is all about. To repent means to change one's mind and to go a different direction.

Recently, I was driving while listening to a podcast. I knew my exit was coming up soon, but I was so absorbed in what the podcasters were saying that I turned off one exit too early. Before I knew it, I was on a limited-access toll road headed in the wrong direction. Realizing what I had done, I desperately wanted to turn around and go the other way, but I couldn't. I had to wait until I reached the next exit. That twelve-mile stretch of road felt like it was one hundred miles long because every mile I drove was taking me further away from my desired destination and costing me time. When I finally got to the exit and turned around, I breathed a sigh of relief, knowing that I was once again headed in the right direction. I had "repented" from my driving error.

When Jesus arrived, he told us that we could experience the full life God created for us to live—if we changed our minds and direction. We can't keep living as we always have and experience the kingdom of God at the same time.

As we follow Jesus, the Holy Spirit will show us when our actions or attitudes are outside of God's will. Then he will call us to repent—to stop living our way and to start living God's way.

So, what does it look like to repent? C. S. Lewis wrote that "Repentance is not something God demands of you before he will take you back . . . it is simply a description of what going back is like."[8]

There are three movements to repentance:

1. Admit that we sinned.

When I took the wrong exit, I needed to admit that I was on the wrong road before I could turn around.

The Holy Spirit will be faithful to open our eyes to where we have taken a wrong turn and sinned. Sometimes that awareness produces an inner stab of remorse; other times, it is just a clear-eyed recognition that something we did or said was outside of God's will. Admitting to ourselves that we have sinned is the first step toward repentance.

2. Confess and ask for forgiveness.

Confess literally means "to say with." When we confess our sin, we "say with" God that we did wrong.

Psalm 32:3–5 describes a prayer of repentance:

When I kept silent,
    my bones wasted away
    through my groaning all day long.
For day and night
    your hand was heavy on me;
my strength was sapped
    as in the heat of summer.

---

8. C. S. Lewis, *Mere Christianity* (New York: HarperOne, 2009), 57.

Then I acknowledged my sin to you
    and did not cover up my iniquity.
I said, "I will confess
    my transgressions to the LORD."
And you forgave
    the guilt of my sin.

When we confess our sins, God forgives us. We don't have to drag guilt around any longer. We don't forgive ourselves; we embrace God's forgiveness.

3. Ask for the power to live God's way.

Repentance starts with changing our minds, which leads us to live differently. Until we do so, we have not repented.

There is an old story about a man who wrote a letter to the Internal Revenue Service explaining that he hadn't been able to sleep well for the last ten years because he had cheated on his income tax. Enclosed in the letter were eight $100 bills. The man concluded the letter by saying that if he didn't sleep better, he would send the rest. That's not repentance; that's just a guilty conscience.

Repentance is not a one-time act; it is a lifestyle. As we follow Jesus, we come to realize that becoming like him involves ongoing change.

▶ Prayer

Lord Jesus, please change any part of me that keeps me from following you with my whole being. Amen.

Day 7

Working It Out

For Individual Reflection

1. **Give thanks to God** for his faithfulness, goodness, and activity in your life.

2. **Pray** Psalm 139:23–24:

   Search me, God, and know my heart;
   *   test me and know my anxious thoughts.*
   See if there is any offensive way in me,
   *   and lead me in the way everlasting.*

Pause and open yourself to anything the Holy Spirit might bring to your attention.

3. **Review your week.**
   a. How did I act on what God told me last week?
   b. Where have I noticed God at work?

4. **Respond.**
    a. What stood out the most from this week's read-
       ings? Where is God asking me to focus my
       attention this week?
    b. What will I do in response?

Group Discussion Questions

1. When you hear the word *holy*, what comes to your
   mind? How closely does that image resemble Jesus'
   character and life?

2. Does pursuing a Jesus-shaped life mean that we will
   lose our individuality and become clones? Why or
   why not?

3. In what ways do you most frequently see your old
   nature show up in your thoughts and actions? How
   would your life be different if your new nature were
   able to win more of the inner battles?

4. On a scale of 1 to 10, how confident are you that you will
   become more like Jesus over the next six months? Why?

5. What pitfalls might we face if we do not realize that it is
   the grace of God that enables us to become like Jesus?

6. Share a time you recently sensed the Spirit's conviction. How does knowing that you are already accepted
   by God change the way you respond?

7. Why is repentance essential to a vibrant spiritual life?

Week 2

The Obedience
of Jesus

And being found in appearance
as a man, he humbled himself by
becoming obedient . . .

— Philippians 2:8

"If you love me, keep my commands."

— John 14:15

Day 8

The Answer Is Yes

▶ **Read Matthew 26:36–42.**

Jeff Lewis was an army specialist with the Eighty-Second Airborne Division when he was ordered to parachute out of a plane. At first glance, this does not appear noteworthy. A paratrooper expects to receive an order like that. But Jeff was not a paratrooper; he was a supply clerk. He had never been to jump school. He had no experience with parachutes. He did not know it, but his order was the result of a clerical error.

Even so, the young supply clerk reported for duty. A short time later, he strapped on a parachute, then when it was his turn to jump, he stepped out of the airplane and started his free fall. Amazingly, he landed unhurt.

When asked later what went through his mind during the experience, he said he was just doing what a good soldier is supposed to do: follow orders. "The Army said

I was airborne-qualified," Lewis said. "I wasn't going to question it."[1]

Those who serve in the military quickly learn to obey orders. The first stop for new recruits is boot camp, where drill sergeants instill in them the habit of instant obedience. There is a good reason for this. In combat situations, officers cannot afford to take the time to explain to their soldiers the rationale behind their orders. While they are taking enemy fire, they can't poll the unit for their opinions or invite discussion. Soldiers must learn to respond, "Sir, yes, sir!" to every order that comes from their commanding officers.

Hebrews 5:8 tells us that Jesus learned to be obedient to his heavenly Father. He consistently said yes to God. Growing in Christlikeness means developing that same habit. There is no such thing as a Jesus-shaped person who does not obey God because Jesus' life was marked by obedience to the Father. (Fortunately, God will never make a clerical error in his commands to us.)

Following Jesus would be a breeze if it were always easy to obey God, but it is not. At times we might want to ask: "This is an exception to that command, right, Lord?" Or we might protest: "That's unrealistic, God!" Sometimes we may be tempted to ignore God altogether.

That is why Philippians 2:8 challenges us to have the same mindset as Jesus, who "humbled himself by becoming obedient to death—even death on a cross!"

The cross is the most powerful example of obedience in Jesus' life. On the night before he was crucified,

---

1. "Parachute School Was a Breeze for This Army Supply Clerk," *Chicago Tribune*, May 20, 2000, https://www.chicagotribune .com/news/ct-xpm-2000-05-20-0005200101-story.html.

Jesus prayed in agony over what lay ahead: "Going a little farther, he fell with his face to the ground and prayed, 'My Father, if it is possible, may this cup be taken from me. Yet not as I will, but as you will'" (Matt. 26:39).

Jesus knew that crucifixion was a horrific, torturous death. He did not want to go through it. He pleaded with God to spare him from it. But in the end, Jesus prayed, "Not as I will, but as you will." He said yes.

Jesus obeyed God even to the point of death. However, most of the time, God is telling us how to live, not how to die. God's commands are not always easy to obey, but his intent is to bless us, not to rob us of joy.

Christlike obedience has two characteristics:

1. Our obedience is to be immediate.

When God commands us to act, the time to do so is now. Don't procrastinate or wait for conditions to be perfect before acting on what God said. Delayed obedience is disobedience. Author Clare De Graaf teaches believers to follow the "10-second rule."[2] That is, as soon as you are reasonably sure of something God wants you to do, commit within ten seconds to do it. That is a good description of the habit of saying yes to God.

2. Our obedience is to be complete.

If you ask your son to put the dishes in the dishwasher and he leaves half of them on the table, you will not say, "Great

---

2. Clare De Graaf, *The 10-Second Rule: Following Jesus Made Simple* (New York: Howard Books, 2013).

job." You'll remind him to do what you asked. In the Great Commission, Jesus told us to make disciples who obey.

> Therefore go and make disciples of all nations, baptizing them in the name of the Father and of the Son and of the Holy Spirit, and *teaching them to obey everything* I have commanded you. (Matt. 28:19–20, emphasis added)

Jesus did not command us to teach people to memorize his words. He did not ask us to gather people to discuss and debate what he said. Jesus instructed us to teach people to obey *everything* he commanded.

A simple way of growing in the habit of obedience is to read the Bible until you come to a command or an example and do it. James 1:22 says, "Do not merely listen to the word, and so deceive yourselves. Do what it says." If we hear what God says but do not do it, we practice self-deception. We believe we are growing spiritually, but we are not. We think we are pleasing God, but unless we do what God says, we are not. Jesus once asked: "Why do you call me, 'Lord, Lord' and do not do what I say?" (Luke 6:46).

Saying yes is the way to a Jesus-shaped life of joy and peace.

▶ Prayer

Holy Spirit, please show me any areas where I am resisting the leading of Jesus. Help me to respond to you completely and immediately. Amen.

Day 9

Simulated Holiness

▶ **Read Matthew 23:24–26.**

If you've ever wondered what it feels like to be at the controls of a Boeing 737 as it takes off or cruises at thirty-five thousand feet, you can now find out. Professional-grade flight simulators cost tens of millions of dollars and are rarely available, as they are in use around the clock to train commercial pilots. However, a few are now open to the public.

After paying a five-hundred-dollar (or higher) fee, you climb into the enclosed cockpit of the simulator. You sit in front of actual flight controls and instruments taken from retired planes. High-definition visuals, surround sound, and vibration combine to create an immersive experience. A certified pilot guides you through the actual flight procedures of takeoff, cruising, and landing.

The flight simulation experience is about as close as you can get to flying a commercial airplane without leaving the ground. Professional pilots find the experience of flying a full-motion simulator to be amazingly accurate, as the entire structure rotates along three axes to create the impression of aircraft movement. Of course, there are obvious differences between a simulator and a real plane. On the upside, you can't kill anyone if you crash in a simulator. The downside is that you don't go anywhere. You go through the motions of flying, but when you climb out of the cockpit, you are just where you started.

We can experience a simulated holiness too. It is called legalism.

In Matthew 23, Jesus confronted the Pharisees over their legalistic ways. The Pharisees were zealous Jews who believed they would please God and gain eternal life by organizing their lives around keeping religious laws. Not only did they focus on keeping the 613 commandments in the Torah (the first five books of the Old Testament), they also created their own laws about those laws, just to be sure they wouldn't break the original laws! They figured that if they kept the rules they created, they would not come close to breaking God's commandments. However, they also devised ways to get around those laws.

For example, God commanded his people to keep the Sabbath day holy by not doing any work (Ex. 20:8–10). Later, rabbis came up with thirty-nine categories of laws about the definition of *work*, such as no carrying objects outside one's home.

That is why today, in certain Jerusalem neighborhoods, there is a wire running overhead called the *eruv*. This wire does not carry electricity; it is a legal loophole for Sabbath-keeping. The eruv is a symbolic fence that gives the designated area the status of a courtyard. It allows residents to leave their houses and carry their baby or a basket to a neighbor's home without breaking the Sabbath law.[3]

Jesus rebuked the Pharisees for focusing on the letter of God's command to tithe while missing God's heart. The Pharisees meticulously tithed (gave 10 percent) of even their garden produce to God, but at the same time, they exploited legal loopholes in order to avoid financially supporting their elderly parents. They kept the law of giving in a technical sense, but they missed God's intent for tithing, which is to help us be generous people. Their legalism was simulated holiness.

In Matthew 5:20 Jesus tells his followers: "For I tell you that unless your righteousness surpasses that of the Pharisees and the teachers of the law, you will certainly not enter the kingdom of heaven."

Jesus' hearers must have wondered: *How can I be more righteous than the Pharisees? I can't keep more laws than they do.*

Jesus was not urging us to keep more laws than the Pharisees did; he wanted us to pursue a holiness of heart rather than mere external compliance. He was saying that rule-keeping is not God's aim; God wants to transform our hearts.

Sin is often a fruit of believing lies and inherited woundedness. Persistent disobedience and warped attitudes are often symptoms of deep brokenness. In an interview with Carey Nieuwhof, seminary professor and

---

3. Illene Prushner, "Snow in Jerusalem: Down to the Wire for Sabbath-Observers," *Haaretz*, December 15, 2013, https://www.haaretz.com/.premium-snowed-in-on-sabbath-in-jerusalem-1.5300665.

counselor Terry Wardle says that after working with thousands of leaders, he is convinced that aberrant behavior is driven by deep wounds, false beliefs, and ungrieved losses.[4] As God heals those inner dysfunctions, our lives will begin to reflect his holiness.

The reason that Jesus could perfectly obey the Father is that his heart was perfectly whole. He did not struggle with insecurity, regret, or bitterness. He was secure in his identity as the beloved Son of the Father, so he was not driven to prove his significance. Therefore, his obedience was natural most of the time because it flowed out of his inner wholeness.

Legalism can never make us holy because it deals only with externals. It fails because it attempts to weed the yard by clipping off the plant tops. Not only do the weeds resurface, but the roots also keep spreading underground and will sprout in another location.

If we measure our spiritual maturity in terms of rule-keeping, we will become either prideful or depressed. We will not become like Jesus either through legalism or by breaking his commands.

The only way to become more like Jesus is to bring him all of who we are, inviting him to heal and change us from the inside out.

▶ Prayer

Lord Jesus, I want to follow you with my whole being. Help me to align my reality with my intentions. Amen.

---

4. "Terry Wardle on Why So Many Leaders Cave," *Carey Nieuwhof Leadership Podcast*, accessed December 21, 2019.

Day 10

Renouncing Sin

▶ **Read Titus 2:11–14.**

A small crowd of demonstrators filled a street in Charlottesville, Virginia. They were protesting against a white nationalist rally that was happening across town. Then, the unthinkable happened. A neo-Nazi sympathizer aimed his car at the cluster of people and stomped on the accelerator. As he plowed into the demonstrators, bodies flew in all directions. One young woman was killed. America watched and gasped. Ken Parker watched and cheered.

Parker was committed to racial hatred. He was a grand dragon in the Ku Klux Klan. He posted on Facebook a photo of himself with a swastika tattoo on his chest and a gun in his arms.

As the nation tried to come to grips with the tragedy in Charlottesville, the makers of a documentary film about hate groups invited Parker to appear as a spokesman for white nationalists. He agreed. The filmmaker, who is a Muslim from Europe, recorded Parker making anti-Jewish flyers and tossing them into front yards.

During the making of the documentary, Parker noticed that the filmmaker was kind to him, not antagonistic. After the film was completed, Parker watched it. He was not comfortable with the man he saw.

Around this time, Parker and his fiancée had a casual conversation with their neighbor, who happened to be the pastor of an African American church in town. The pastor also treated the couple with kindness and invited them to worship.

Parker and his fiancée attended a service and felt welcomed by the congregation's members. So, they attended another service. Soon, they were regular attenders at All Saints Holiness Church.

Even so, Parker felt he could not leave the brotherhood of the National Socialist Movement (NSM), a neo-Nazi party. He still planned to attend an upcoming rally in Georgia. However, the night before he was to leave, he prayed for guidance. In the end, he decided not to go to the rally. Instead, he sent a resignation email to the NSM. "I could not keep living that lifestyle of hate," Parker said.

Almost a year after he marched as a neo-Nazi in Charlottesville, Ken Parker walked into the Atlantic Ocean with his black pastor, was lowered under the water, and rose to a new life. A few days later, he began the process of having his white supremacist tattoos removed. Parker turned his back on racial hatred and embraced Christ.[5]

What an eloquent picture of the renunciation of sin. Ken Parker cut all ties with the groups he had previously

---

5. Monica Rhor, "He Was a KKK Member, Then a Neo-Nazi: How One White Supremacist Renounced Hate," *USA Today*, November 1, 2018.

supported. All of us who seek a Jesus-shaped life are called to cut ties with our sins by renouncing them.

Titus 2:11–14 says:

> For the grace of God has appeared that offers salvation to all people. *It teaches us to say "No" to ungodliness* and worldly passions, and to live self-controlled, upright and godly lives in this present age, while we wait for the blessed hope— the appearing of the glory of our great God and Savior, Jesus Christ, who gave himself for us to redeem us from all wickedness and to purify for himself a people that are his very own, eager to do what is good. (emphasis added)

When we renounce our sin, we say no to what is not like Christ and we embrace his ways. Renouncing sin goes beyond admitting our faults. We can admit we've done wrong, yet still not commit to change. To renounce sin, we declare that we are making a clean break with it.

Some years ago, I had the privilege of attending a naturalization ceremony as one of our church's members became a US citizen. Those becoming US citizens take this oath:

> I hereby declare, on oath, that I absolutely and *entirely renounce* and abjure all allegiance and fidelity to any foreign prince, potentate, state, or sovereignty, of whom or which I have heretofore been a subject or citizen; that I will support and

defend the Constitution and laws of the United States of America.[6] (emphasis added)

To become US citizens, people renounce their previous nation's citizenship. They no longer have any allegiance to that country; they pledge their loyalty to the United States instead.

When we renounce sin, we declare that we no longer have anything to do with it. The baptismal liturgy of the United Methodist Church includes this question:

On behalf of the whole Church, I ask you: Do you renounce the spiritual forces of wickedness, reject the evil powers of this world, and repent of your sin?[7]

Sin won't go away on its own; we need to send it away. To be free from sin, we need to choose to renounce it. Titus 2 tells us that the first step is to make the decision to say no. Verse 12 says that it is God's grace that "teaches us to say 'No' to ungodliness." Choosing to reject sin is the first step toward freedom.

If we want to hang on to a pet sin, God will not force us to let go. He will prompt us, even convict us, but he won't compel us against our will. He gives us a choice as

---

6. "Naturalization Oath of Allegiance to the United States of America," U.S. Citizenship and Immigration Services, updated July 5, 2020, https://www.uscis.gov/citizenship/learn-about-citizenship/the-naturalization-interview-and-test/naturalization-oath-of-allegiance-to-the-united-states-of-america.
7. General Board of Discipleship of the United Methodist Church, *The Services of the Baptismal Covenant in the United Methodist Church* (Nashville: The United Methodist Publishing House, 2009).

to whether we want to live under his leadership or sin's domination.

Have you made the choice to renounce sin? If not, why not do so today?

▶ Prayer

In the name of Jesus, I renounce and reject the sin(s) of _____ that has/have a hold on me. Amen.

Day 11

When You're Offered the World

▶ Read Matthew 4:8–10.

I was walking through a grocery store when an employee asked me: "Would you like to try a free sample?" He was pointing to a plate of sushi. Since I am not a fan of raw fish, I smiled and said, "No, thank you," and kept walking. (Now, if he had offered me some quality gourmet cheese, that would have been a different matter.)

Stores know about the power of temptation. Marketing research reveals that when a grocery store pumps the smell of fresh bread into the air, it triples the sales in their bakery department. The aroma lures us to taste.

Satan tried to entice Jesus to worship him:

Again, the devil took him to a very high mountain and showed him all the kingdoms of the world and their splendor. "All this I will give you," he said, "if you will bow down and worship me."

> Jesus said to him, "Away from me, Satan! For it is written: 'Worship the Lord your God, and serve him only.'" (Matt. 4:8–10)

We can be eternally grateful that Jesus did not buy what Satan was selling. If he had given in to temptation, Jesus could not have died for our sins because he would have committed his own.

Satan wants to derail God's plan for our lives too. The devil seeks to distort our lives so that they look nothing like Jesus', and temptation is one of the devil's favorite tools to accomplish this. But we do not need to fall for his false promises. God can empower us to resist the lure.

Temptation is a choice; it is not a sin. We know this because Jesus was tempted, yet he was without sin (Heb. 4:15). Temptation is a fork in the road where we can choose God's way or another way.

When we are tempted, we need to remember that temptation's attractiveness is based on a deceptive sales pitch. For example, Satan told Jesus, "If you worship me, then you'll get all the kingdoms of the world." Satan didn't mention that any power Jesus would derive from worshiping him would be short-lived. Not only that, but God would give Jesus more authority than Satan ever could:

> Therefore God exalted him to the highest place
>> and gave him the name that is above
>>> every name,
> that at the name of Jesus every knee should bow,
>> in heaven and on earth and under the earth,
> and every tongue acknowledge that Jesus Christ
>> is Lord,
>>> to the glory of God the Father. (Phil. 2:9–11)

Temptation lies to us, whispering that we will be happiest and most fulfilled when we ignore God and his ways. That is simply not true. God is not holding out on us. He is not trying to keep us away from the good stuff of life. God wants to fulfill our legitimate desires in a healthy way.

Satan enticed Jesus to turn stones into bread. Jesus' hunger was a legitimate need. However, Satan was tempting him to fulfill that need illegitimately. That would dishonor God and constitute a misuse of his power. Satan also tempted Jesus with authority. Each of us has a legitimate desire for significance. The problem was that Satan was tempting Jesus to fulfill that need through idolatrous means.

Psalm 34:8 says, "Taste and see that the LORD is good." When we are tempted, our best defense is to focus on the goodness of God—to run to his love, his provision, his mercy, his arms.

Bryan Chapell writes about the day his wife, Kathy, and a friend took their children for an afternoon outing at the Saint Louis Zoo. While there, they decided to visit Big Cat Country, an area of the zoo where the lions and tigers roamed in large enclosures while visitors observed them from elevated skyways above the habitats.

Kathy and the kids were walking on the skyway ramp when a blanket became entangled in the wheel of the friend's stroller. When Kathy stopped to untangle the blanket, her boys—ages three and five—kept going. When Kathy looked up, she saw that the boys had walked right through a child-sized gap in the fencing and had climbed up on the rocks some twenty or twenty-five feet above the lion pen. Pointing to the lions below, they called back to their mother, "Hey, Mom, we can see them!"

They had no concept of how much danger they were in. However, Kathy realized it immediately. Her mind raced through her options. If she screamed, she might startle the boys perched precariously above the lions. The gap in the fence was too small for her to get through. So, she knelt, spread out her arms, and said, "Boys, come get a hug." They came running for the love that saved them from danger greater than they could perceive.[8]

First Peter 5:8 says, "Be alert and of sober mind. Your enemy the devil prowls around like a roaring lion looking for someone to devour." One of the ways he does that is by trying to convince us that he will treat us better than God will. But that's a lie. When we face temptation, let's run to the goodness of God, who will give us the power to resist.

▶ Prayer

Lord, help me to not buy the lies that temptation sells. Amen.

---

8. Bryan Chapell, *Holiness by Grace: Delighting in the Joy That Is Our Strength* (Wheaton, IL: Crossway, 2001), 107.

Day 12

Stubborn Sin

▶ **Read Romans 6:15–18.**

In her book *Acedia & Me*, Kathleen Norris writes:

> I have become like the child I once knew who
> emerged one morning from a noisy, chaotic
> Sunday-school classroom to inform the adults
> who had heard the commotion and had come to
> investigate, "We're being bad, and we don't know
> how to stop."[9]

Have you ever admitted to yourself: "I am being bad,
and I don't know how to stop"? If so, you are not alone.
All Christ-followers have experienced the frustration of
knowing that what we are doing is sin and being unable
to stop. Even the apostle Paul once lamented: "For I do
not do the good I want to do, but the evil I do not want to
do—this I keep on doing" (Rom. 7:19).

---

9. Kathleen Norris, *Acedia & Me: A Marriage, Monks, and a
Writer's Life* (New York: Riverhead Books, 2008), 16.

Some sins seem to drop away from us quickly as we grow spiritually. Others, though, cling stubbornly to our souls, resisting our best efforts to free ourselves. The saints from the past used to call these *besetting sins*, or *strongholds*.

The term *stronghold* refers to a fortified military outpost that is difficult to conquer. That is an apt name for a stubborn sin. Some sins are strongholds because they exert a strong hold on us. They vary from person to person. For one, it might be explosive anger; for another, it might be unbridled lust or greed or envy.

Our specific sin may vary, but our battles with strongholds follow a predictable and recurring pattern.

First, we recognize that an attitude or action is sinful—for example, exploding in anger. So, we determine not to lose our temper again. For a while, all is well. We go several days without an outburst. We remain composed. But then, after an exhausting day at work, we come home to find two of our small children writing on the walls. We explode, red-faced and loud. An hour later, we feel guilty, knowing we've sinned again. We ask God's forgiveness, vowing to him and to ourselves that we will never blow up again. Then, after a few days of tranquility, something else triggers us, and our anger erupts all over those nearest to us. Once again, we feel ashamed and ask God's forgiveness and help not to do it again. Repeat ad nauseam. We are in the grip of a stubborn sin.

It is confusing. We may have been able to stop committing other sins through prayer and discipline. But this one is different; it won't budge. Are we doomed to live under the tyranny of this sin, or is there a way out?

Author Tony Stoltzfus suggests that when prayer-fueled discipline fails to bring freedom, it is likely because we have an unmet legitimate desire that we are trying to fulfill in our own power.

He observes that we are all driven by the core desires of achievement, connection, competence, and stability. I would call these needs because they are necessary for us to live the abundant life Jesus offers us. These basic needs generate in us deep motivations such as love, security, approval, significance, and more.[10]

Our actions are driven by these needs, often without our knowing it. For example, a compulsion to acquire and hoard money might be motivated by our need for security or significance. These core desires are not evil, but if we seek to meet them apart from God, we will be driven to sin. The sinful greed that keeps us from being generous might be driven by a fear of losing our security. Once we learn to find our security in God, it becomes easier to give as God commands.

Sometimes we misidentify our needs. We think we need a drink, so we go to the bar and end up drunk. But our deeper need is not a drink; it is peace. We think we need sex and thus end up in the wrong person's bed. But, in fact, our true need is love and acceptance.

Holiness is not about training ourselves to deny our deepest needs; it is about letting God meet them. James 4:1–2 says:

> What causes fights and quarrels among you? Don't they come from your desires that battle within you? You desire but do not have, so you kill. You covet but you cannot get what you want,

10. Tony Stoltzfus, *The Invitation: Transforming the Heart through Desire Fulfilled* (Redding, CA: Coach22, 2015), 60ff.

so you quarrel and fight. You do not have because you do not ask God.

James is not saying that it is wrong to desire. Rather, he implies that God will fulfill the legitimate desires of our hearts if we ask him. Then we will not be compelled to fill them in our own distorted way.

Jesus looked to God to meet his core needs. For example, when Satan tempted him to meet his legitimate need for food in an illegitimate manner, Jesus responded: "Man shall not live on bread alone, but on every word that comes from the mouth of God" (Matt. 4:4). Jesus was able to resist temptation because his core desire of communion with God was fulfilled. At the right time, he was able to eat dinner in a God-honoring manner. Jesus consistently let God meet the core desires of his life, and that allowed him to live a perfectly God-honoring life.

Can we actually find freedom from sin by fulfilling our deepest needs? Isn't that selfish? Didn't Jesus teach us to deny ourselves and follow him?

Jesus taught us to deny our urge to live by our own direction and resources; that is, to fulfill our needs our way. Denying ourselves does not mean denying our need for significance any more than it means denying our need for food. God created us with the need to eat as well as with the need for significance. When those needs are met in God-honoring ways, we are connected more closely to him, not alienated from him like we are in sin.

If you are struggling with a stubborn sin, ask yourself what unmet desire lies behind it. Until it is met by God, your sin will exert a stubborn hold on you. Invite God to show you how to meet that need in a way that will honor him. He created you to have needs, and he will meet them in a healthy way.

▶ Prayer

Lord, help me to understand my deepest needs and let you meet them. Amen.

Day 13

Inside-Out Living

▶ **Read Matthew 5:21–30.**

Clauvino "Shorty" da Silva was a gang leader in one of Brazil's oldest criminal groups when authorities arrested him for drug trafficking. He was sentenced to seventy-three years and ten months in a Brazilian prison.

In 2013, he managed to escape his cell through the sewer system and immediately returned to his gang's violent activities. He and three accomplices dressed up in police uniforms and attempted an armed takeover of a drug-running operation in Rio de Janeiro. They were arrested and sent back to jail.

A few years later, da Silva made international headlines when he attempted to escape from prison by switching clothes with his teenage daughter, who had come to visit him. He put on her pants, shirt, and glasses, and then pulled on a silicone mask and a black wig. Guards were not fooled by the disguise, though. When he tried to leave, they apprehended him and took him to a more secure facility.[11]

Da Silva proved that putting a police uniform on a drug runner will not make him a law enforcement officer. Dressing a gang leader in his daughter's clothing will not make him a high school girl. No matter how da Silva changed his appearance, he was still the same person. Changing his appearance did not change his inner nature.

A Jesus-shaped life does not consist of reforming external actions; it is the result of a transformed heart. Becoming like Jesus goes far deeper than training ourselves to behave in acceptable ways; it is about taking on the inner nature of Jesus. God wants to do more than modify our behavior; he wants to renovate our hearts, which is what motivates our actions.

In the Sermon on the Mount, Jesus told us that God looks beyond our actions and sees the state of our hearts.

For example, in Matthew 5:21–22, Jesus says:

> You have heard that it was said to the people long ago, "You shall not murder, and anyone who murders will be subject to judgment." But I tell you that anyone who is angry with a brother or sister will be subject to judgment.

God does not want us to murder. But God's best goal for us involves more than just not killing someone. He wants our inner lives to match our outer behavior.

Similarly, Jesus upped the ante on sexual integrity:

---

11. Igor Derysh, "Clauvino da Silva: 5 Fast Facts You Need to Know," *Heavy*, accessed September 28, 2019, https://heavy.com /news/2019/08/clauvino-da-silva/.

> You have heard that it was said, "You shall not commit adultery." But I tell you that anyone who looks at a woman lustfully has already committed adultery with her in his heart. (vv. 27–28)

Christlikeness goes beyond not sleeping with someone else's wife. A husband who avoids physical contact with other women while regularly ogling them and looking at pornography is not fulfilling God's intent for marital faithfulness.

Jesus is emphasizing that holiness is lived from the inside out. However, he is not teaching that our actions and our thoughts are morally equivalent. There is a vast difference between thinking, *I could kill him*, and literally committing murder. Each falls short of God's intent for us, but they carry very different consequences. Although all sins separate us from God, all sins are not equal in terms of the damage they inflict. Physical murder destroys lives to a far greater degree than an angry attitude does. The physical act of adultery wreaks greater havoc on a marriage and family than a lustful look does.

Jesus did not just preach the Sermon on the Mount; he lived it. If he did not, it would have been nothing more than a poetic but irrelevant collection of words. Jesus taught us not to seek "an eye for an eye" revenge. He said, "Do not resist an evil person. If anyone slaps you on the right cheek, turn to them the other cheek also" (v. 39). We could dismiss that as an unrealistic ideal, except for the fact that Jesus did what he taught when he allowed tormentors to strike him and insult him as they prepared to execute him.

And Jesus didn't just sermonize about forgiving our enemies; he forgave his. While he was hanging from the cross, he forgave those who nailed him to it. He not only said, "Pray for those who persecute you" (v. 44), he also prayed, "Father, forgive them" (Luke 23:34), as he hung dying on the cross. Jesus practiced what he preached. His actions were consistent with his words.

One of the ways we can measure the degree of our inner transformation is by how consistently our words match our actions. If our actions do not reflect what we say we believe, it shows we have not yet been transformed inwardly. Our inner character becomes visible through our actions and words. True, Jesus is the Son of God in a way that we are not. However, we are God's children (John 1:12), and he has given us his Holy Spirit to empower us to live like Jesus.

Spiritual practices like prayer, fasting, and gathering in small groups are vital because they open our inner beings to the shaping work of the Holy Spirit. As you read and reflect on this devotional, you are inviting the Lord to shape you in Jesus' image from the inside out.

▶ Prayer

Lord, help me to live out what I say I believe. Amen.

Day 14

Working It Out

For Individual Reflection

1. **Give thanks to God** for his faithfulness, goodness, and activity in your life.

2. **Pray** Psalm 139:23–24:

   Search me, God, and know my heart;
   *   test me and know my anxious thoughts.*
   See if there is any offensive way in me,
   *   and lead me in the way everlasting.*

   Pause and open yourself to anything the Holy Spirit might bring to your attention.

3. **Review your week.**
   a. How did I act on what God told me last week?
   b. Where have I noticed God at work?

4. **Respond.**
    a. What stood out the most from this week's readings? Where is God asking me to focus my attention this week?
    b. What will I do in response?

Group Discussion Questions

1. What possible honest answers might someone give to the question Jesus asks in Luke 6:46: "Why do you call me, 'Lord, Lord,' and do not do what I say?"

2. Why is it contradiction to say, "Jesus is my Lord," and not obey him?

3. Why is legalism attractive on a certain level? Why is it spiritually deadly?

4. What is the difference between regretting a sin and renouncing it?

5. On a scale of 1 to 10, how loved by God do you feel right now? Unless it is a 10, pray for each other to be filled with more of his love.

6. Share a time you successfully resisted a temptation. What were the keys to victory?

7. Is there an issue in your life you've given up trying to change because you've been unsuccessful? What is God saying to you about that right now?

8. Take a moment to pray for each other to be filled with the Holy Spirit.

The Relationships of Jesus

"Greater love has no one than this: to lay down one's life for one's friends."

—John 15:13

And let us consider how we may spur one another on toward love and good deeds, not giving up meeting together, as some are in the habit of doing, but encouraging one another—and all the more as you see the Day approaching.

—Hebrews 10:24–25

I used to want to fix people, but now I just want to be with them.

—Bob Goff

Day 15

What Counts

▶ **Read 1 Corinthians 13:1–7.**

During the 2004 Olympics, Matthew Emmons held a commanding lead in the fifty-meter three-position rifle final. After nine shots, all he had to do was hit somewhere around the bull's-eye, and he would win the gold medal. For a marksman like him, it was almost impossible to fail.

Preparing for his last shot, Emmons reminded himself to calm his body to avoid any unforced errors. He later said, "I came down on the target . . . *boom*— shot the shot—then looked at the TV monitor, and there's nothing there."[1]

It turned out that Emmons had aimed at the target in Lane Three, when he was assigned Lane Two. He had made an excellent shot at the wrong target. That gave him a score of zero, which moved him from first to eighth place.

---

1. Ollie Williams, "London 2012: Is Matt Emmons America's Unluckiest Olympian?," *BBS Sport*, June 7, 2012, https://www .bbc.com/sport/olympics/18348092.

Can you imagine how frustrating that would be? Imagine training for years, only to lose the gold medal by shooting at the wrong target. That would be crushing.

As frustrating as making that mistake would be, aiming at the wrong target in life would be even worse. Imagine coming to the end of our lives and discovering that nothing we did ultimately counted. We don't have to experience that, though, because God has clearly marked our life's target.

We have seen that Jesus said that the two greatest commandments are (1) to love God and (2) to love others. Today, let's consider the second part of our bull's-eye: love for others.

First Corinthians 13:1–3 tells us:

> If I speak in the tongues of men or of angels, but do not have love, I am only a resounding gong or a clanging cymbal. If I have the gift of prophecy and can fathom all mysteries and all knowledge, and if I have a faith that can move mountains, but do not have love, I am nothing. If I give all I possess to the poor and give over my body to hardship that I may boast, but do not have love, I gain nothing.

This passage reminds us that our lives will be measured in eternity by the way we love. Our success on earth won't be measured by our fame, our wealth, or even by the good works that we've done. It is love that makes our lives count. Everything else is secondary.

Love is the distinguishing characteristic of a Jesus-shaped life.

Genuinely loving others with our actions and attitudes will honor God and inoculate us against sin.

At one point, members of the early church were arguing about whether or not a Christian was required to be circumcised in obedience to the Mosaic law. The apostle Paul reminded them: "For in Christ Jesus neither circumcision nor uncircumcision has any value. The only thing that counts is faith expressing itself through love" (Gal. 5:6).

If we have hearts filled with love, we don't need a thousand laws to keep us in line. When we love others, we will not lie to them, steal from them, or attack them. That's why Jesus said all the Law and the Prophets hang on the two commandments to love God and love others (Matt. 22:40).

A Jesus-shaped life isn't focused on avoiding sin; holiness is the fruit of loving others. When we are motivated by love, our words will be life-giving. Whatever we do with our talents and spiritual gifts will accomplish God's purposes. Our sacrifices will make an eternal difference when we make them out of love.

Jesus had all the abilities listed in 1 Corinthians 13. He could speak with angels. He could fathom all mysteries. He had mountain-moving faith, and he gave himself to the poor. He gave his body to be crucified and killed. But the reason it mattered to us was that he did it out of love. He loved the Father and he loved us enough to die for us.

So how do we increase our love for others? It doesn't work to grit our teeth and try harder. We love others when we feel loved ourselves. We can't give what we do not possess. Thankfully, God loves us more than we can fathom. Ask God to show you his love for you, and then your love will overflow to others.

Facing eternity has a way of eliminating clutter and revealing what is important.

When former president George H. W. Bush died in 2018, people from all across the political spectrum attended his funeral. Notable figures eulogized his life. Some alluded to his accomplishments, but most remembered his character—his kindness and his integrity.

His son, former president George W. Bush, spoke about what he remembered most about his father. He recalled that the elder Bush loved his wife, Barbara, fiercely and that his last words to his son were simply, "I love you."

What a strong reminder of what counts most in life. Both men had been president of the United States when historic events occurred. The father had been the director of the CIA. He was vice president when someone attempted to assassinate the president. He was president when the Berlin wall fell and the Soviet Union dissolved. The son had been president when our nation was attacked by terrorists on 9/11. Both men led wars in the Middle East.

But at the end, they didn't even mention any of that. What the world considers most important didn't matter at all. When we're getting ready to step into eternity, all the distraction and fluff melts away. Only what ultimately counts remains. And what counts is love.

▶ Prayer

Lord, please show me your love so that I can love others deeply from my heart. Amen.

Day 16

Forgiving Others

▶ **Read Acts 7:57–60.**

The young man stood serenely in front of the hostile, agitated crowd. Those venting their displeasure at him were no common rabble. Most of the men were members of the Sanhedrin—the select group of rabbis who comprised Jerusalem's tribunal.

The authorities had detained Stephen after some synagogue members had accused him of blasphemy. There was no question about whether he was a follower of Jesus of Nazareth. It was public knowledge that he was a member of the new sect called "the Way." It was also well known that he organized the sect's daily distribution of food to the group's widows. Some citizens were sympathetic to him because they said he healed people and performed unexplainable miracles. But others argued with Stephen, trying to convince him to renounce Jesus and return to the ways of their fathers.

Their efforts failed, though, so now Stephen was the Sanhedrin's headache. The officials charged Stephen with blasphemy and gave him a chance to respond. Incredibly, instead of defending himself against such a serious charge, he preached to them. Stephen traced Israel's history from its beginning to the moment Jesus died and rose again. Then he dared to conclude by declaring that the Sanhedrin had helped get Jesus killed. To top it all off, he announced that he saw Jesus standing at the right hand of God. The Jewish leaders found that to be intolerable. They determined that Stephen had to be punished—by death.

The crowd around the Sanhedrin was growing larger. Onlookers became vocal as the atmosphere of indignation and rage intensified. "Stone him!" they screamed. There was no turning back now. The mob surrounded Stephen and started pushing him toward the edge of town. It was clear how this was going to end.

The mob dragged Stephen through the streets by his clothing until they were outside the city gates. Arriving at a suitable spot, the crowd shoved Stephen to the ground and surrounded him. The men scrambled to pick up rocks; some of them were the size of a fist so they could be hurled at great speed, while others were so large that it took two arms to lift them above their heads.

Then the assault began. The smaller rocks rained down on all parts of Stephen's body. Blood began to stain the ground. Stephen knew he was about to die. He saw men approaching with massive stones held aloft, ready to inflict the final crushing blows that would end his life. Stephen cried out in prayer, but he didn't pray for himself; he prayed for those who were killing him. "Lord, do not hold this sin against them" (Acts 7:60). Those were the last words he spoke before he stepped into the presence of Jesus.

Stephen forgave the men who were killing him. Where did he get the idea to do such a thing? Why did that occur to him? Stephen was echoing Jesus' words from the cross: "Father, forgive them, for they do not know what they are doing" (Luke 23:34). Stephen not only lived a Jesus-shaped life, he died a Jesus-shaped death. He forgave those who persecuted him, just as Jesus did.

Forgiving others is a distinguishing mark of a Christ-follower. It requires supernatural strength to look at someone who intentionally abuses and hurts us and to say, "I forgive you," especially when they are not asking for forgiveness.

A Jesus-shaped life has no room for grudges. Following Christ means forgiving others, just as we've been forgiven by God. Jesus taught us to pray, "Forgive us our sins, for we also forgive everyone who sins against us" (Luke 11:4).

If we are going to forgive others, we need to know what forgiveness is and what it is not.

Forgiveness is not pretending that we were not hurt. When we forgive someone, we acknowledge that we have been wounded.

Forgiveness is not making excuses for the other person, as in, "They didn't mean to hurt me." Sometimes the other person did mean it, yet we still are called to forgive. The guards didn't nail Jesus to the cross by accident, but he forgave them.

Forgiveness is not the same thing as reconciliation. Sometimes we forgive people with whom we will no longer have a relationship.

So, what is forgiveness? Forgiveness is releasing the right to get even. Anne Lamott said, "Forgiveness means it finally becomes unimportant that you hit back. You're done."[2] It is saying, "You hurt me, but I will not hurt you in return. I will leave the scales unbalanced."

Forgiveness is ultimately unfair; it is choosing not to give the other person what they deserve. Aren't you glad that God forgives you instead of giving you what you deserve?

When we're struggling to forgive, it helps to remember that we have offended God. We have hurt him by our behavior. Even though he gave us life, untold blessings, and opened heaven to us, we have sinned against him. And yet, God has fully forgiven us. He will not try to get back at us for hurting him. We are called to treat others the same way.

Miriam lives in the Middle East and came to Christ out of a Muslim background. Starting when she was seven years old, her father regularly raped her. This horrific abuse continued through her late teens. Yet when she came to faith in Christ, she said, "If God forgives all that people have done against him, then I can forgive my father." Only the power of God makes this kind of forgiveness possible.

Forgiving others is not a burdensome duty for those who want a Jesus-shaped life; it is a path to freedom from bitterness. We live among imperfect people, so we all get hurt at times (some people more than others). But Jesus can free us from carrying grudges that ruin our health and steal our joy. He will empower us to forgive.

---

2. Anne Lamott, *Plan B: Further Thoughts on Faith* (New York: Riverhead Books, 2006), 47–48.

▶ Prayer

Father, thank you for forgiving me. Please make me willing to forgive those who hurt me, especially the person I now name in my heart. Amen.

Day 17

Look Closer

▶ **Read 2 Corinthians 5:16–21.**

As our three boys grew up, it became increasingly challenging for my wife and me to hide their Christmas presents. Our house wasn't big, so there weren't many secret places available. Then my wife, Linda, came up with a plan. As she purchased gifts, she would put them in cardboard boxes labeled "Old Clothes." The kids might have seen those boxes, but they never looked inside. (At least, they never told us they did!) Because of the label, they assumed the box held nothing that interested them.

That's the problem with labels: they are not always accurate, especially when it comes to people.

People have been labeling one another for thousands of years. From the early Egyptians to the medieval English to the citizens of any nation today, people of every culture label others. It seems to be human nature. Today, Americans use a variety of labels to categorize each other. We label others according to their income, race, and political affinity. We identify people by their accents, their jobs, their nation of origin, and even their sports team loyalties (Go Penguins!).

Yet, all of these categories are human inventions. It was not God's original intent that we divide ourselves into camps that ignore or oppose each other. Jesus commanded us to love one another, not label one another. It is hard to love people when we label them because, by labeling them, we reduce them to a stereotype and do not see them for who they truly are. We miss the gift inside because we make assumptions about them.

A young man I know was working as a management trainee at a rental car company. One day a wealthy customer made small talk at the counter by talking about his recent trip to Florence, Italy.

"It is a beautiful city," he said. "If you can ever afford it someday, you should go." As it happens, my friend had been to the city five times with his father. So, he responded to the customer: "Did you stay near the Ponte Vecchio or in another part of the city?" Shocked, the customer said simply, "Oh." That customer had labeled my friend and assumed he could never have been to Florence.

Jesus saw beyond people's labels and treated each person as valuable. While Jews saw Samaritans and women as groups to avoid, Jesus defied convention and struck up a conversation with a Samaritan woman. Jews were taught that Gentiles were religiously unclean, but Jesus healed Gentiles and commissioned his disciples to preach the gospel to all nations. To grow in Christlikeness is to see others as Jesus did.

The apostle Paul said that knowing Christ changes the way we look at people. In 2 Corinthians 5:16a he said, "So from now on we regard no one from a worldly point of view." After Paul started to follow Jesus, he stopped categorizing people. He looked beyond surface traits. He admitted that before he became a Christian, he even labeled Jesus. At one time, Paul looked at Jesus as a misguided heretic. Paul later discovered that he was wildly wrong. "Though we once regarded Christ in this way, we do so no longer" (v. 16b).

The church is the family of God. It is one place where society's labels should never matter. After we become Christ-followers, any other label becomes secondary. Second Corinthians 5:17 says, "Therefore, if anyone is in Christ, the new creation has come: The old has gone, the new is here!" When we put our trust in Christ, we become new creations—children of God. The old categories are gone, and our new identity is what describes us most accurately. Anyone in Christ is a new person and can no longer be categorized by any other label.

As we look around at work, school, or the store, rather than seeing people as Republicans or Democrats, Hispanic or white, let's look closer to see their real identities. Be very careful about referring to someone by a label, such as Mexican/black/white/liberal/conservative, or making general statements about groups, such as "Democrats are . . ." or "Republicans always . . ."

To live a Jesus-shaped life, we need to see people as God does. That is, we need to recognize that *every person is a creation of God.*

Whether or not they are followers of Jesus, every person you meet is a uniquely crafted creation of God. It has been aptly said, "You have never locked eyes with someone who is not created and loved by God." Jesus died for each person you saw today, whether they know it or not. Your auto mechanic, your cousin, and your congressperson are each created by God and, therefore, infinitely valuable. Viewing people this way will influence the way we treat them.

Some people are *children* of God. A certain percentage of the people you will see today are not only creations of God, they are also part of God's family. It is not accurate to say, "We're all children of God." We are all created by God, but only those who put their faith in Jesus are God's children. John 1:12 says, "Yet to all who did receive him, to those who believed in his name, he gave the right to become children of God."

Each person we meet is on the way to an eternity either with or without Christ. C. S. Lewis urges us to open our eyes to this spiritual reality:

> Remember that the dullest and most uninteresting person you talk to may one day be a creature which, if you saw it now, you would be strongly tempted to worship, or else a horror and a corruption such as you now meet, if at all, only in a nightmare. All day long we are, in some degree, helping each other to one or other of these destinations. It is in the light of these overwhelming possibilities, it is with the awe and circumspection proper to them, that we should conduct all our dealings with one another, all friendships, all loves, all play, all politics. There are no *ordinary* people. You have never talked to a mere mortal.[3]

▶ Prayer

Lord, help me see the people around me as you do. Amen.

---

3. C. S. Lewis, *The Weight of Glory* (New York: HarperOne, 2001), 45–46 (emphasis in original).

Day 18

Good Sex

▶ **Read 1 Thessalonians 4:1–8.**

"I have had sex, and Jesus still loves me."

Hannah Brown's statement is one of the more memorable lines in the history of ABC's reality TV show *The Bachelorette*. In case you are not familiar with the program, its premise is that a single woman dates multiple men over several weeks in hopes of finding her true love. In the final episode, one of the remaining two bachelors is expected to propose.[4]

When Brown was the bachelorette, Luke Parker, one of the contestants, raised the issue of waiting to have sex until marriage. Both of them professed to be Christians, but it soon became apparent that they had very different perspectives on chastity. Parker was dismayed when Brown told him that she had had sex with other

4. Holly Thomas, "'I Have Had Sex, and Jesus Still Loves Me' Wins 'Bachelorette' Argument," CNN, July 18, 2019, https://www.cnn.com/2019/07/17/opinions/the-bachelorette-sex-argument-luke-hannah-thomas/index.html.

contestants on the show, and he let her know of his disappointment. Brown was offended by his response and sent him packing.

Brown later told an interviewer, "Regardless of anything that I've done, I can do whatever, I sin daily and Jesus still loves me. It's all washed and if the Lord doesn't judge me and it's all forgiven, then no other man, woman . . . anything can judge me. Nobody's gonna judge me; I won't stand for it."[5]

It appears that Brown believes that her sexual activity is irrelevant to her relationship with God. She can do whatever and Jesus still loves her.

Why does that sound both right and wrong?

It is true that the Bible says that God loves us even when we sin: "God demonstrates his own love for us in this: While we were still sinners, Christ died for us" (Rom. 5:8). At the same time, authentic faith in Jesus always leads us to want to become like him. And the Bible says that our sexual behavior matters to God.

First Thessalonians 4:3 says, "It is God's will that you should be sanctified: that you should avoid sexual immorality."

God's purpose for us is that we become holy; that is, like Jesus. And Jesus avoided sexual immorality (which includes any sexual activity that is outside of God's moral boundaries).

5. Charity Gibson, "Bachelorette on Show's Sexual Relations: 'I Can Do Whatever, I Sin Daily and Jesus Still Loves Me,'" *Christian Post*, June 19, 2019, https://www.christianpost .com/news/bachelorette-on-shows-sexual-relations-i-can-do -whatever-i-sin-daily-and-jesus-still-loves-me-231708/.

Verse 4 reveals that God's will is "that each one of you should learn to control your own body in a way that is holy and honorable."

The church has too often left the impression that God's will regarding sex can be summed up as "Don't," or even as "Sex is dirty and disgusting, and you should save it for the one you love." That is ridiculous and untrue.

Sex is God's idea, and it is good. Like many of God's good gifts, it has been misused and even twisted. However, God designed sex to create a unique bond between a married couple. It is part of the two becoming one (Matt. 19:5).

Good sex is chastity in singleness and faithfulness in marriage between a man and a woman. It is holy and honorable to abstain from sex until we are married and then to enjoy sex with our spouse once we are married.

Today, however, holding to this standard will mark us as different—maybe even odd. That should not be surprising, though. The word *sanctified* literally means "to be set apart." And make no mistake about it, following God's ways when it comes to sexuality will set us apart. Verse 5 alerts us that we are to act "not in passionate lust like the pagans, who do not know God." In our Western culture, following God's ways regarding sex may be one of the most distinctive marks of a Jesus-follower. Abstaining from sex before marriage is considered quaint at best and unhealthy at worst. That is nothing new; the ancient Romans thought the first Jesus-followers were strange and superstitious because they limited sex to marriage.

Tertullian was a second-century church leader who wrote a defense of Christianity. In explaining Christians to a pagan audience, he pointed out that Christ-followers are generous and share their resources. He said, "One in mind and soul, we do not hesitate to share our earthly goods with one another. All things are common among us *except our wives.*"[6] He highlighted this exception because it was common for pagan Roman men to share their wives with other men. Roman society also accepted prostitution, pedophilia, and a low view of women. They thought it odd that Christians did not share their perspective.

It is not easy to follow God's will for sex, and we will stand out when we do. People around us will not understand and may even ridicule us. Sexual purity may be one of the most countercultural aspects of being a Jesus-follower in America today. But it is worth it.

What we do with our bodies impacts our spiritual health. Adopting the world's moral standard will hurt us spiritually, relationally, and even physically. It will prevent us from growing to love and obey Jesus as completely as we might. It will hinder our ability to hear God's voice clearly, and it will reduce our confidence in taking bold steps of faith.

We do not need to resign ourselves to a life of spiritual defeat, though. When we ask the Lord to forgive us, he does. (Hannah Brown was right about that!) In Isaiah 1:18 God says, "'Come now, let us settle the matter,' says the LORD. 'Though your sins are like scarlet, they shall be as white as snow; though they are red like crimson, they shall be like wool.'"

God always gives us the power to do what he calls us to do. He will help us to stop conforming to the world and

---

6. *Ante-Nicene Fathers. Volume 3: Latin Christianity: Its Founder, Tertullian*, eds. Alexander Roberts, James Donaldson, and A. Cleveland Coxe (New York: Christian Literature Publishing Co., 1885), 46.

to start yielding to the Holy Spirit. We can trust that God loves us and leads us toward what is best, which includes avoiding sexual immorality.

▶ Prayer

Lord, I offer you my body as a living sacrifice. Give me the power to live for you even if everyone around me goes a different direction. Amen.

Day 19

For Every Age

▶ Read 1 John 2:12–14.

I felt conspicuous and uncomfortable as soon as I walked into the church. I have been a pastor for a long time, so I am usually quite at ease in worship environments. But not that morning. I was uneasy because the congregation consisted primarily of college students, and I was in my early fifties. When I chose to worship there that morning, I didn't realize that this church's average age would be twenty-two years old. After looking around, I felt like a guy bringing a hamburger to a vegan picnic. I braced myself for raised eyebrows and an unspoken, "What are you doing here?"

To their credit, everyone was accepting and welcoming. However, that morning I was reminded of why the church needs to be a mixture of all generations.

Most of us gravitate to people our own age because we feel most comfortable around people who are like us. Interacting with people much younger or older than us can seem like encountering foreigners. Sometimes people even write off other generations as incomprehensible. Baby boomers shake their heads and murmur, "Millennials want a trophy for everything," while millennials dismiss their parents' peers with, "Okay, boomer," as if they can't even engage with someone who is so out of touch.

But the church is the family of God, and every generation is important. If we want to become like Jesus, we need the contributions of people of every age.

The apostle John was a teenager when he started following Jesus. He lived to be a senior citizen in his nineties, becoming the only one of the twelve apostles to live to old age. When John was nearing the end of his life, he wrote the letter that we now call the book of 1 John. In it, he speaks to different generations in the church:

> I am writing to you, dear children,
>> because your sins have been forgiven on
>> account of his name.
> I am writing to you, fathers,
>> because you know him who is from the
>> beginning.
> I am writing to you, young men,
>> because you have overcome the evil one.
>
> I write to you, dear children,
>> because you know the Father.
> I write to you, fathers,
>> because you know him who is from the
>> beginning.
> I write to you, young men,
>> because you are strong,
>> and the word of God lives in you,
>> and you have overcome the evil one.
>> (2:12–14)

It is spiritually unhealthy to assume that believers of a different age group have nothing to offer us. Each generation has a strength that the others need. The spiritual children need to know how to overcome the evil one like the young men do. The young men who overcome the evil one need to know the eternal God like the fathers do. We need each other.

I have been following Jesus for forty-two years now. The faith that I had as a single, eighteen-year-old college freshman was different from the faith I had fifteen years later as I was planting a church and raising three young boys. My core doctrine was consistent, but my experiences shaped the way I trusted God, how I handled both joys and sorrows, and my understanding of God's will. Now that I have passed age sixty, I have lived through even more. My relationship with God continues to deepen. At each stage, I had strengths that I could offer to the body of Christ, as well as needs the church could meet.

Often, the young in our churches have the boldness to take major risks for the gospel. They are more available to help plant churches or serve overseas. Older generations need the example and encouragement of the young in order to keep taking risks of obedience.

Older generations have already encountered the challenges younger people are going through, and they know where the landmines are buried. They may not be as tech-savvy, but they have navigated challenging seasons of life and stayed close to Jesus. Younger generations need their example and encouragement.

Our spiritual maturity is hindered when we associate only with people our own age. We need the influence of all the generations of the body of Christ. So, if you are younger, invite an older person to dinner. Ask them to share their stories or tell you about how they make decisions. If you are older, invite a younger person to your house for dinner. Ask about what is going well in their lives and what concerns they have. Let them know you believe in them and their ability to make a difference. Encourage them to trust God for more. Be honest with them about your successes and failures.

Some say that older people should let younger people take over leadership of the church. While senior leaders certainly need to make room for young leaders, the church is strongest when all generations serve and lead together. Who will mentor the younger generation if the older one doesn't? And how will the church reach the next generation unless the younger believers are contributing to the mission? You are never too old or too young to make a difference in someone else's life.

Recently, my wife and I worshiped at a newly planted church. The average age of the congregation was around twenty-five years old. The preacher was wearing the classic millennial church planter uniform of ripped jeans, chains, and flannel. I loved his passion and the urgency of his message. Toward the end of his sermon, he urged (maybe looking at us?): "If you are older, please come back. We need you!"

The apostle John would say "amen" to that.

▶ Prayer

Father, give me the opportunity to be influenced by all the generations in your family. Amen.

Day 20

A Passion for God

▶ **Read Matthew 22:36–40.**

When I was a kid, I was a fanatic about baseball. My friends and I would play ball until we couldn't see in the dark. My parents allowed me to pull out the hedges and transform our backyard into a ball field—pitcher's mound and all.

I ate, slept, and thought baseball. It was a major event whenever I had the chance to go to a Pirates game. Every time I entered the ballpark and saw the field, I felt awe and wonder. My first paying job was as a baseball coach. I had a *passion* for baseball.

Maybe you had a passion like that when you were growing up—something that consumed you: a favorite band, favorite sport, animal, or a passion for fashion—something that made others wonder if you were a little over the top in your dedication.

Today, I still enjoy baseball, but I have to admit that I am not as passionate as I used to be. Maybe it's because the game has changed, and I have too. Maybe it's because I realized whether the Pirates come in last or win the

World Series won't change what matters most (though I'd still like to see them in the Series!).

So, what matters most?

One day some Pharisees asked Jesus what mattered most to God:

> "Teacher, which is the greatest commandment in the Law?"
>
> Jesus replied: "Love the Lord your God with all your heart and with all your soul and with all your mind." This is the first and greatest commandment. (Matt. 22:36–38)

Love God with all your heart, soul, strength, and mind. That sounds like passion, doesn't it? Jesus is saying that passion for God and love for others is what matters most. Notice he did not say, "Believe in God." There is a big difference between belief and passion.

The idea of being passionate for Jesus makes some people nervous. They fear it might mean becoming fanatical or intolerant. Not so! Having a passion for Jesus won't make us religious freaks or plastic people. It will, however, shape our lives in positive ways.

When we have a passion for God, we become more content. When we are hungry for God, he delights in satisfying us.

Texas pastor Bob Roberts struggled with the lack of growth at his church. One day in his frustration, he went out to a hillside near his house and complained to God. Why wasn't his church growing like other ones he knew? He sensed God reply: "Bob, when will Jesus be enough for you?" That day, Bob determined that Jesus was enough. If he never had a big church, that was okay as long as he knew Jesus. If no one outside his church ever knew his name, he would be just fine with that. As it turned out, Bob's church did grow. Today, he influences business, government, and spiritual leaders around the world. But what satisfies Bob most is knowing Jesus.

When we have a passion for Jesus, he is more than enough. We may have goals, but we pursue them with contentment.

When I was in seminary, Linda and I lived in an apartment that was located directly below that of Dr. J. C. McPheeters, who was a former president of the seminary. He was more than ninety years old at that time, yet his passion for Jesus was overflowing. People told me that when Dr. McPheeters met with God in prayer early each morning, he could be heard down the hallway. Even with his door shut, fellow residents said they heard him praying, singing, and shouting, "Praise the Lord!"

I was a twenty-three-year-old student at the time and thought: *Wow, I want to have that kind of fire when I'm old!* Dr. McPheeters had a spring in his step, a smile for everyone, and an energy that came from being lit up by love for God. He radiated love for Jesus until God took him to heaven.

Where did Dr. McPheeters get that passion? And where can we get some? We do not work for spiritual passion; we receive it. It is not a religious achievement. Passion is not something we accomplish; it is a response to God's love.

First John 4:19 tells us: "We love because he first loved us." When Jesus' love melts our hearts, then passion for him will grow. When it dawns on us how much he loves us, our natural reaction will be to love him back. He loves us so much more than we can possibly imagine. There's nothing we can do to earn it. God loves you just as much on the days you sin or ignore him as on the days you feel like you've hit all the marks.

Ask God to reveal his love for you. If you want to be filled with God's presence, put yourself under his faucet. That is, make yourself available to him through prayer, worship, and any other way you connect with him.

Passion for Jesus won't wear off like my baseball passion. The more you experience his love, the more you will want to love the one who loved you first.

▶ Prayer

Lord, please show me how much you love me. Amen.

Day 27

Working It Out

For Individual Reflection

1. **Give thanks to God** for his faithfulness, goodness, and activity in your life.

2. **Pray** Psalm 139:23–24:

    Search me, God, and know my heart;
    *   test me and know my anxious thoughts.*
    See if there is any offensive way in me,
    *   and lead me in the way everlasting.*

Pause and open yourself to anything the Holy Spirit might bring to your attention.

3. **Review your week.**
    a. How did I act on what God told me last week?
    b. Where have I noticed God at work?

4. **Respond.**
   a. What stood out the most from this week's readings? Where is God asking me to focus my attention this week?
   b. What will I do in response?

Group Discussion Questions

1. If we asked those around you, how high would they say showing love ranked on your priority list last week: highest priority, somewhat of a priority, or not much of a priority?

2. How can you tell if you have forgiven someone who hurt you?

3. Share a time you were labeled. How did it make you feel?

4. Why do you think God calls us to live celibate before marriage and to be faithful in marriage? How does this affect us spiritually?

5. Share how someone of another generation has helped you grow spiritually. What steps could you take to mentor or to be mentored by someone of another generation?

6. Has your passion for God been increasing or decreasing over the last three months? What step would God have you take?

The Courage of Jesus

Then Jesus was led by the Spirit into the wilderness to be tempted by the devil.

—Matthew 4:1

Jesus took the Twelve aside and told them, "We are going up to Jerusalem, and everything that is written by the prophets about the Son of Man will be fulfilled. He will be delivered over to the Gentiles. They will mock him, insult him and spit on him; they will flog him and kill him. On the third day he will rise again."

—Luke 18:31–33

Day 22

Set Apart

▶ **Read 1 Peter 2:11–12.**

One day I was cutting some paper when Linda asked: "Which scissors are you using?" When I held them up to show her, I was surprised that her eyes grew wide with alarm.

"You're using my good fabric scissors! Never cut paper with fabric scissors; you'll ruin them!"

I had no idea. I figured that scissors were scissors and that one pair was as good as any other when it came to cutting. I discovered otherwise.

All of us routinely set apart certain items for exclusive use. For example, I have a pair of dress shoes in my closet. I only wear them when I am wearing a suit (which is to say, not very often). I would never think of wearing them to cut the grass or to work out. Some people have good dishes that they use only for special occasions or decorative towels that they would never use to wash their windows.

A Jesus-shaped life is one that is set apart for God. In other words, it is holy. To be holy means to be set apart or dedicated to God. Holy ground is different from other places because it is dedicated to God. And holy people are set apart for God.

First Peter 1:15–16 says, "But just as he who called you is holy, so be holy in all you do; for it is written: 'Be holy, because I am holy.'" Here the writer is quoting the Old Testament book of Leviticus, where God tells the Jews, "I am the LORD, who brought you up out of Egypt to be your God; therefore be holy, because I am holy" (Lev. 11:45).

When God brought the Jews out of slavery in Egypt, he gave them laws to set them apart as his special people. Obeying those civil, ceremonial, and moral laws made them different than the rest of the pagan cultures that surrounded them. That uniqueness is one of the reasons God gave dietary laws to the Jews. We might wonder why God cared whether his people ate pork or shellfish. One answer is that adhering to a kosher diet served as a practical, daily reminder that they were to be different from the people of other nations. It set them apart at every mealtime.

First Peter 2:9 tells us Christ-followers: "But you are a chosen people, a royal priesthood, a holy nation, God's special possession, that you may declare the praises of him who called you out of darkness into his wonderful light."

Through faith in Jesus, we become God's chosen people, holy and set apart. Our uniqueness does not stem from a kosher diet. As Christ-followers, we can eat ham sandwiches if we are so inclined. That is because after the resurrection of Jesus, the apostles recognized that the Old Testament dietary laws were no longer binding for non-Jews (Acts 15). The ceremonial laws had been fulfilled in Jesus. And the Jewish civil laws do not apply to us because we do not live in a theocracy (where priests rule in the name of God) like Israel did.

Instead, we are to stand out as different because of our Christlike character. First Peter 2:11–12 exhorts us:

> Dear friends, I urge you, as foreigners and exiles, to abstain from sinful desires, which wage war against your soul. Live such good lives among the pagans that, though they accuse you of doing wrong, they may see your good deeds and glorify God on the day he visits us.

When we live Jesus-shaped lives, there will be times we act differently than most people. We might even feel like foreigners and exiles, like we're from another place.

I was driving through the western Pennsylvania countryside one day when I came upon a horse and buggy driven by an Amish couple. As I carefully passed them, I had to admire their willingness to live differently than the rest of the world. Although I don't find any evidence in the Bible that driving a car displeases God, I do see plenty of other directives in Scripture that will make us stand out as we follow them.

For example, God calls us to live with a different sexual ethic than the rest of society does. We are to handle power in a Christlike way, which is not the norm. We will use our time and money differently. We may treat immigrants or the unborn more respectfully than others do. We are to love more freely and forgive more quickly.

Jesus' followers have always stood out as different from the cultures in which they lived. That is not easy to do. It takes courage to dance to a different song than everyone else.

I live in a beautiful part of the country, and there are several lazy rivers just a short drive away from my house. On most sunny summer afternoons, those rivers are dotted with people in inner tubes floating gently down-stream at a leisurely pace. There is no need to paddle or steer; the current does all the work.

Other nearby rivers are not so lazy. Their currents move quickly, and jagged rocks jut out from the surface, creating white water. There, people don't just float down the river; they paddle purposefully in order to maneuver between rocks and to shoot the rapids. If they lie passively and let the current take their raft wherever it wants, they will likely end up tossed overboard or pushed against (or under) large rocks.

We cannot unthinkingly go with the flow of the culture and still live a Jesus-shaped life. Living for Christ requires intentional navigating. We cannot simultaneously follow Christ and the crowd. As God's people, we will sometimes stand out because of our actions. That is what it means to be set apart as holy.

The reason Linda did not want me to use her fabric scissors to cut paper is that they would lose their cutting edge and become unusable for their intended purpose. A willingness to be different allows us to keep our cutting edge and to fulfill God's purpose for us. It takes courage to stand out and live a Jesus-shaped life.

▶ Prayer

Lord, give me the courage to follow you instead of the crowd. Amen.

Day 23

Think Differently

▶ **Read Romans 12:1–2.**

Alex and Rhoda Toth and their six children had less than twenty-five dollars to live on for the next seven days. Their prospects looked bleak, as they had already been living on beans, rice, and canned soup for weeks.

Then Alex hit the jackpot—literally. He bought the winning ticket in a Florida lottery drawing worth thirteen million.

The Toths declared the money would not change their lives, but it did. They spent the next three months living in a thousand-dollar-a-night hotel room in Las Vegas. They gambled, dined, shopped, and bought tickets to expensive live shows. After their splurge, the Toths returned to Florida. They purchased ten acres of property and a double-wide trailer and settled there with their family.

But they did not live happily ever after. The Toths ended up filing for bankruptcy—twice. They became so broke that their only electricity came from a wire that ran to their car engine. They were convicted of filing three years of fraudulent tax returns. On top of that, Alex was arrested multiple times for growing marijuana and writing bad checks. He died penniless while awaiting trial, while Rhoda was sentenced to two years in prison for tax evasion.[1]

It seems hard to believe that someone who won millions in the lottery could end up with nothing. But sadly, the Toths are not unique. Studies show that winning the lottery does not save people from financial trouble; it often leads people into deeper holes. Three to five years after their wins, bankruptcy rates for lottery winners are far higher than those of the general population.[2] The winners' bank balances change, but their thinking about money doesn't. They are presented with large amounts of money, but they end up where they started because they don't change the way they deal with money.

Most of us will not win the lottery, but it is easy to think that our lives would be different if our circumstances changed:

"If only I had more friends, I would be happier."

"If I didn't have so much stress at work, I would be more peaceful."

"I could be more like Jesus if my spouse were more spiritual."

However, genuine change is not a result of our circumstances; it flows from our thinking. Romans 12:2 says, "Do not conform to the pattern of this world, but be transformed by the renewing of your mind."

---

1. "Rags to Riches Fairytales Gone Bad: The Alex and Rhoda Toth Story," https://www.lottoexposed.com/the-alex-and-rhoda-toth-story/.

2. Abigail Johnson Hess, "Here's Why Lottery Winners Go Broke," August 25, 2017, https://www.cnbc.com/2017/08/25/heres-why-lottery-winners-go-broke.html.

Personal transformation comes from changing our thinking. That is because our thoughts steer our lives.

On one of our date nights, Linda and I went to the theater to see one of the *Lord of the Rings* movies. During tense scenes, when the good guys were in danger, Linda gripped my hand the way an alligator clamps on a fish. When a monstrous spider appeared on the screen, she covered her eyes and asked me to tell her when it was gone. I appreciated her using both hands to cover her eyes because, otherwise, I might never have regained the use of my hands! The vivid images on the big screen were producing emotional reactions in us. We were reacting to what filled our minds.

That happens even when we are not at the movies. Every day, we react to life according to what fills our minds. Our actions begin as thoughts.

We need our minds renewed because we can't live like Jesus if we think like the devil. We can't enjoy a life of peace, faith, power, and love while our minds are filled with doubt, fear, bitterness, and resentment. To live a Jesus-shaped life, we must be transformed by the renewing of our minds.

Monitoring what we watch and hear helps us do that. Media (all types) is one of the primary tools of conforming us to the world's value system. Americans spend an average of just more than four hours per day watching TV and more than two hours on their phones with social media and other apps.[3] That's a massive intake

3. Quentin Fottrell, "People Spend Most of Their Waking Hours Staring at Screens," August 4, 2018, https://www.marketwatch.com/story/people-are-spending-most-of-their-waking-hours-staring-at-screens-2018-08-01.

of opinions and values that are often opposed to God's truth. Six and a half hours every day translates to more than twenty-three hundred hours per year of absorbing the values promoted by advertisers, movie scripts, song lyrics, and celebrities.

We need to be realistic. If we spend 2,300 hours per year absorbing society's values and, say, 52 hours per year (an hour per week) taking in God's truth, it is obvious which influence will shape us most. We will be conformed to the culture far more than to Jesus' image.

I am not proposing that we unplug our televisions and throw away our phones. I am suggesting that we monitor what we view and hear. Watch and listen critically. Where does the movie promote something God prohibits? When are the lyrics assuming something different than what God says is true? It takes intentionality to develop a discerning eye and ear.

To recognize God's truth, we must take it in. Spending time with him in worship, Scripture, and prayer allows the Spirit access to our hearts and minds. That leads us toward a Jesus-shaped life.

By reading this book you are doing just that. You are letting God's truth shape your thinking. And by participating in a small group, you are letting other Christ-followers influence you in positive ways. Don't let yourself be shaped primarily by TV, an app, or even your friend group. Instead, "be transformed by the renewing of your mind" (Rom. 12:2).

▶ Prayer

Lord, fill my mind with your reality as I spend time with you each day. Amen.

Day 24

Though None Go with Me

▶ **Read 2 Timothy 3:10–17.**

"Glory to Jesus!" the young woman shouted as she raised her arms heavenward. Her white dress was dripping as she emerged from the swimming pool. A small crowd clapped their hands and joined her in shouting praise to God. The woman was the first new believer baptized that Sunday morning in Syria, but she wouldn't be the last. Fifteen others lined behind her, waiting to be immersed.

One after another, newly converted men and women descended the pool's stairs to be baptized. The pastor prayed for each in turn and then gently plunged them under the water. Each believer emerged to the sound of loud applause and a warm embrace.

After all sixteen converts were baptized, the group broke into worship, singing:

I have decided to follow Jesus;
I have decided to follow Jesus;
I have decided to follow Jesus;
No turning back, no turning back.

In Syria, those words are not just aspirational lyrics. As Linda Lowry wrote, "Those singing it know that their decision to follow Jesus comes with a great price. If, or when, their conversion is discovered, these new believers could lose their family, friends, their job, even their lives." Following Jesus will turn their lives upside down.

> The world behind me, the cross before me;
> The world behind me, the cross before me;
> The world behind me, the cross before me;
> No turning back, no turning back.

Believers in Syria know that becoming a Christian means leaving their old life, their old world, and their old religion behind them. And in front of them is a cross—a symbol of persecution.[4]

Today, one out of nine Christians worldwide experience high levels of persecution. Hundreds of millions of people around the world live in nations where it is illegal to follow Jesus.

Believers in the underground church of China worship secretly. Almost all of their key leaders spend time in jail at least once. In parts of the Middle East the persecution is extreme. In North Korea, anyone discovered with a Bible or worshiping Jesus is brutally persecuted and usually killed. Christians are crucified, hanged from bridges, drowned, or burned alive.[5] Worldwide, 4,136

---

4. Linda Lowry, "For 16 Syrian Believers, Baptism Is a Radical Choice," Open Doors USA, February 25, 2019, https://www.opendoorsusa.org/christian-persecution/stories/for-16-syrian-believers-baptism-is-a-radical-choice/.
5. Father Philippe Blot, "Witness to the Persecution of Christians in North Korea," Keeping the Faith Alive, April 5, 2017, https://www.churchinneed.org/witness-persecution-christians-north-korea-2/.

Christians were killed for their faith during the twelve months preceding November 2018.

Those of us who live in the United States can be thankful that we do not know what it is like to face that kind of persecution. I know that I am grateful. When I was a new believer, I used to wonder: *How would I respond if I was threatened with death for my faith in Jesus? If my family were targeted, would I remain faithful?*

Eventually, I learned that those questions are irrelevant because I am not facing that level of persecution. God prepares and equips us for what we actually face, not for what we imagine. Right now, my task is not to die for Jesus; it is to live for Jesus.

That doesn't mean it will be easy though. Second Timothy 3:12 warns us: "In fact, everyone who wants to live a godly life in Christ Jesus will be persecuted."

No one cares about what we secretly believe; they only object to what they see. And following Jesus makes a difference in our actions. That means that if we want to live a Jesus-shaped life, we can expect to face some sort of opposition from the society around us.

In the United States, Christianity has lost its privileged place in society. Though Christ-followers are not jailed or killed, we are not as favored either. You might not lose your job because you follow Jesus, but you might not get invited to the after-hours get-together if you become known as a Jesus-type. It might not always be possible to retain our coworkers' positive opinion of us and follow Jesus at the same time.

Our society will not encourage us to live a Jesus-shaped life. In overt and subtle ways, it will pressure us to conform to the thinking and the values of the majority. How will we respond? Will we blend in, or will we be willing to stand out? Will we respond to the Spirit's prompt to share with our coworkers how Jesus changed our lives or play it safe and stay quiet? Will we stand our moral ground or go with the crowd?

"The world behind me, the cross before me."

Our brothers and sisters around the world can inspire us to follow with courage. American pastor David Platt visited an Asian country in which following Jesus is difficult. Christians there struggle daily for food, water, and medicine. They are also persecuted for their faith.

Platt wrote about a church service he attended there that moved him deeply. Most of the believers walked for up to two hours to the house where the meeting was being held. The church's pastor had been orphaned when he was fifteen and his non-Christian parents died. A few years later, he became a follower of Jesus when someone shared the gospel with him. As soon as he was baptized, the rest of his family turned their backs on him. He lost the inheritance his parents had left for him. Yet, that did not deter him. He said, "Jesus is worth losing your family." During the service, a young man told the church that he had shared the gospel with someone who reacted by threatening his family with harm. Other members sought to encourage him by sharing their experiences with persecution.[6]

"The world behind me, the cross before me."

---

6. David Platt, *Something Needs to Change: A Call to Make Your Life Count in a World of Urgent Need* (Colorado Springs: Multnomah, 2019), 102–3.

It takes courage to live a Jesus-shaped life. Ask the Holy Spirit, and he will grant you what you need for today's challenges.

▶ Prayer

Lord, keep the cross before me and the world behind me. Amen.

Day 25

Comfort or Christ

▶ **Read Luke 9:23–27.**

What is one thing we must do every day in order to be a disciple of Jesus?

Some might say "pray." That's not a bad answer since we need to be in communication with Jesus in order to follow him. Others might say "read the Bible," or "help the poor," or "show love," or "worship." All of these responses are good ones.

According to Jesus, to be his disciples, the one thing we must do daily is die. Luke 9:23 says, "Then [Jesus] said to them all: 'Whoever wants to be my disciple must deny themselves and take up their cross daily and follow me.'" Jesus said that if we want to be his disciples, we must take up our cross daily.

In Jesus' day, the cross was not a piece of jewelry; it was an instrument of death. The Romans used crosses to execute their enemies. When people saw a cross set up in their town, they immediately thought: *Someone is going to die today.*

When Jesus said that his disciples must "take up their cross," he was saying that they must die. Americans don't need to die physically to follow Jesus, as some in other countries might. Rather, we need to die to ourselves—that is, put aside our intentions and follow his instead.

To die to ourselves means to treat our preferences like a dead person would. Ask a corpse: "What do you want to do today?" They won't tell you. (They won't even say, "Nothing.") Ask: "What do you want to eat?" They won't answer. Dead people have no preference.

Jesus said his disciples "*must* deny themselves and take up their cross daily and follow me" (emphasis added). The cross is not optional. To stay in step with Jesus, we must die to ourselves every day, not just once in a while.

I had the privilege of meeting Pastor Dion Robert several years ago. He pastors a church in Côte d'Ivoire in Africa. His church has more than 200,000 people in cell groups, so he's a pretty good leader. The person introducing him said, "Pastor Dion has a wonderful way of smiling while he tells his people that they need to die." Pastor Robert preaches about dying to self because he is making disciples, not just converts.

Where the church is persecuted, it is growing. One reason for that is that persecution forces people to choose between following Jesus and living a self-directed life. They realize that they cannot do both. And when people choose to follow Jesus instead of their own inclinations, the power of God is released.

Choosing to die to self requires courage because it is rarely comfortable. I admit that I like to be comfortable. I have a La-Z-Boy recliner in my living room. It's set up where I can see the TV, listen to music, and easily reach my stack of books. Sometimes when my dog is lying on my legs, it is so comfortable that I ask Linda: "Could you please bring me a glass of water?" And because she is so kind, she does.

But there are some things Linda can't bring me while I'm in my chair. I can't ask her: "Honey, can you bring me a faster time in next month's 5k?" No, for that, I'll have to get out of the chair and start training. I can't ask her: "Please bring me two new friends." I'd have to choose to get out of my comfortable chair and start connecting with people for that.

Craig Groeschel said, "I like comfort, but comfort never made me more like Jesus." God's abundant life lies outside our comfort zone. So much of what he wants to do in us requires that we stretch. I can't say, "Jesus, will you make me a generous person while I keep all my money for myself?" It doesn't work like that. I can't say, "Jesus, I don't want to risk saying anything about you to my friends because they might mock me. So, will you go ahead make them Christians while I act just like them?"

Jesus challenges us to die to our comfort and follow his call.

Shortly after John Wesley came to faith in Christ, he started to preach about faith in Jesus. But the church leaders of his day ridiculed and rejected him and his message. They banned him from speaking in any Anglican church. Wesley could have chosen to blend in and be accepted by the ruling class of the day. After all, they were the ones who controlled the nation's money and opportunities. He could have decided to keep his spiritual experiences and beliefs to himself. But he didn't. He decided that if he was not allowed to preach in churches, he would take the gospel to the people by preaching in town squares, coal mines, and fields.

As a result, Wesley was ridiculed and persecuted for decades. People threw rocks at him while he preached and dragged him off of the tables he stood on to speak. Sometimes they beat him. But he never complained about the abuse or got preoccupied with it. Wesley's daily journal entry for May 21, 1750, reads: "I rode on to Bandon. From three in the afternoon till past seven, the mob of Cork [a neighboring town] marched in grand procession and then burned me in effigy near Dant's Bridge."[7]

That's all he wrote. He wasn't fazed by angry mobs burning him in effigy. He simply kept doing what Jesus called him to do.

On the night before Jesus was crucified, he wrestled with whether to obey the Father. Should he die on the cross or choose comfort and avoid it? He prayed, "My Father, if it is possible, may this cup be taken from me. Yet not as I will, but as you will" (Matt. 26:39).

Jesus died to his own desires and followed the Father's purposes. The result was the salvation of the world. To live a Jesus-shaped life is to choose to lay down our right to a self-directed life and to choose Christ over comfort.

▶ Prayer

Lord, so fill me with your presence that you become what is most precious in my life. Amen.

---

7. John Wesley, *The Works of John Wesley*, 3rd ed., vol. 1 and 2 (Grand Rapids, MI: Baker Books, reprinted 2007), 188.

Day 26

Lust-Proofing

▶ **Read Matthew 5:27–30.**

As our plane taxied to the gate, the man in the seat next to me pulled out his phone and turned off airplane mode. The glow of his screen caught my eye, and I noticed that his phone's wallpaper was a picture of his wife and two young daughters. Then, he deftly clicked over to another screen and several pornographic pictures appeared. He briefly gazed at the images and then turned his phone off.

The contrast struck me: the smiling faces of his young daughters and the graphic pictures of someone else's daughters. I doubt he saw any connection between the two screens. I'm reasonably sure that he believed that looking at porn had nothing to do with the fate of his wife and daughters. But it does.

Pornography use affects marriages. Research shows that divorce rates double when people start watching pornography.[8]

And make no mistake about it, Americans are viewing pornography. If you wonder why I would devote a chapter to the issue of pornography, consider what one secular reporter found:

> We [Americans] dedicated well over four and a half billion hours to watching porn on one porn site in 2016. Humanity spent twice as much time viewing porn in a year as it has spent existing on planet Earth. It all adds up to over 500 thousand years-worth of porn consumed in the span of 12 months. Since 2015, human beings have spent one million years watching porn. One million years.
>
> I'm telling you this not only because it's an interesting bit of trivia . . . but because these figures are serious. More than serious: staggering, incomprehensible, unthinkable, apocalyptic. All the more so for Americans, because we watch more porn than anybody else on earth.[9]

The revenues of the sex and porn industry in the United States are larger than the NFL, NBA, and Major

---

8. David Shultz, "Divorce Rates Double When People Start Watching Porn," *Science*, August 26, 2016, https://www.sciencemag.org/news/2016/08/divorce-rates-double-when-people-start-watching-porn.
9. Matt Walsh, "We're a Nation of Porn Addicts. Why Are We Surprised by the Perverts in Our Midst?" *The Daily Wire*, November 30, 2017, https://www.dailywire.com/news/walsh-were-nation-porn-addicts-why-are-we-matt-walsh.

League Baseball combined. That makes porn America's favorite pastime.

And the church is participating too. About 68 percent of men in the church regularly watch porn, and 25 percent of married women seek it out at least once per month. They are all aware that Jesus said, "You have heard that it was said, 'You shall not commit adultery.' But I tell you that anyone who looks at a woman lustfully has already committed adultery with her in his heart" (Matt. 5:27–28).

I am certain that you already know that we do not grow in Christlikeness by staring at images designed to enflame our lust. If you are dabbling in porn, I pray that this chapter will be the prompt you need to help you stop. It is not harmless. It wrecks relationships and careers, not to mention it damages our relationship with God.

However, many have tried to quit and have failed. If that is you, understand that my purpose is not to condemn, shame, or embarrass anyone who watches pornography. My goal is to help, restore, and encourage.

No one views porn because they want to promote human trafficking or distort their perspective of sexuality. People watch it because they buy into its lie; namely, that it will make them happy. However, ex-porn star Traci Lords told Dateline NBC: "I can tell you from personal experience that I've never met a happy porn star."[10] And it creates dysfunction in users.[11]

---

10. "Secrets & Lies—Traci Lords," *Dateline NBC*, July 11, 2003.
11. "Watching Pornography Rewires the Brain to a More Juvenile State," *Neuroscience News*, December 29, 2019, https://neurosciencenews.com/neuroscience-pornography-brain-15354/.

Pornography use can become a powerful trap. But God has the power to set us free.

Titus 2:11–14 says:

> For the grace of God has appeared that offers salvation to all people. It teaches us to say "No" to ungodliness and worldly passions, and to live self-controlled, upright and godly lives in this present age, while we wait for the blessed hope— the appearing of the glory of our great God and Savior, Jesus Christ, who gave himself for us to redeem us from all wickedness and to purify for himself a people that are his very own, eager to do what is good.

Let me offer four beginning steps toward freedom for all who are trapped in pornography.

1. Embrace God's love.

Habitual porn use is fed by inner wounds, needs, and emptiness. It is often an attempt to numb pain or distract from fear. Porn is a symptom, not a cause.

If you are using pornography, hear this: God loves you! He loves you not only when you are successfully resisting, but even when you fail miserably. He loves you when you are at your lowest moment. God's love for you does not depend on your moral performance. Romans 5:8 says, "But God demonstrates his own love for us in this: While we were yet sinners, Christ died for us." If you have any desire to be free from porn, God will help you do so.

Titus 2:12 tells us that salvation (a right relationship with God) will teach us to say no to destructive passions. It might take some trial and error to learn, but God loves us enough to teach us.

Remember, God's purpose for you is not merely to keep you away from pornography, it is to help you know him more deeply.

2. Confide in a fellow believer.

Pornography addiction thrives on isolation. And isolation intensifies shame, which, in turn, further isolates people. It is a vicious cycle. However, you can break that cycle by speaking the truth aloud to another Christ-follower. If you are thinking: *I'll try to do it myself first, and if that doesn't work, then I'll tell someone*, let me ask you: How has that strategy worked so far?

James 5:16 says, "Confess your sins to each other and pray for each other so that you may be healed." You don't need to announce your struggle to the world; just find one safe person and confess. We're only as sick as our secrets.

We can hear the truth that God loves us, but we need to experience that love in order to be healed. We need someone to look us in the eye and say, "I know what you did, and I love you anyway." We need to feel their embrace to be able to believe the truth that God loves us in spite of our sin.

3. Install safeguards.

Everyone who owns a computer knows they need a virus protection program. If you surf the Internet without one, it won't take long for your computer to start running poorly and perhaps fail altogether.

Accessing Internet pornography will destroy something more valuable than your computer; it can wreck your marriage, mind, relationships, and the abundant life God offers. Just as we install virus protection software on all our computers, every device we own should have a pornography filter. Find it online and install it.

4. Focus on the life God offers.

God's highest goal for you is not that you would avoid porn; it is that you experience the abundant life of joy, peace, and love that Christ died to purchase for you. He has a freer, richer life in store for you than what the screen offers. When you taste the goodness of life with Jesus, you will not settle for the destructive illusion of porn.

The Lord loves you and will bring you freedom if you do not give up.

▶ Prayer

Lord, please make me pure in heart. Help me to focus my eyes only on what will build my love for you and others. Amen.

Day 27

Resisting Money's Orders

▶ **Read 1 Timothy 6:6–10.**

Philip Yancey is a Christ-follower who has wrestled with how to deal with money. He once wrote:

> I feel pulled in opposite directions over the money issue. Sometimes I want to sell all that I own, join a Christian commune, and live out my days in intentional poverty. At other times, I want to rid myself of guilt and enjoy the fruits of our nation's prosperity. Mostly, I wish I did not have to think about money at all.[12]

But we do have to think about money, don't we? We don't have the luxury of ignoring it. We must deal with it daily. And if we are going to live a Jesus-shaped life, we must deal with it in a healthy way. Money is like food; we need it to survive, but an unhealthy relationship with it will hurt us.

---

12. Quoted in Gordon MacDonald, "Becoming a Generous Giver," Preaching Today, https://www.preachingtoday.com/sermons/sermons/2012/december/becoming-generous-giver.html.

The apostle Paul warned us: "Some people, eager for money, have wandered from the faith and pierced themselves with many griefs" (1 Tim. 6:10b). If not handled well, money can erode our relationship with God and produce pain. Conversely, using money under the influence of the Holy Spirit can lead to tremendous good. What makes the difference?

First Timothy 6 tells us that money will hurt us when it wins our affections: "For the love of money is a root of all kinds of evil" (v. 10a).

Notice that it is not money itself that is the source of problems; it is a faulty relationship—the love of money—which is the root of all evil.

On Tuesday, September 8, 2015, a British Airways jet caught fire at the Las Vegas airport. The left engine had a catastrophic failure, sending smoke billowing into the air. Flames were creeping dangerously close to the Boeing 777's fuselage.

As the plane burst into smoke and flames and the aircraft was ordered to evacuate, onlookers noticed something astonishing. Some of the passengers were stopping to grab their luggage out of the overhead bins. The FAA requires planes to be evacuated within ninety seconds. If just half of the people on board took the time to take their bags, the evacuation would have taken seven minutes longer than necessary. One blogger summarized: "People love their carry-ons more than life itself."[13]

Before boarding that plane, none of those passengers would have said that they value their bags more than

13. "Passengers Love Their Bags More Than Life," Preaching Today, https://www.preachingtoday.com/illustrations/2015/october/7100515.html.

their lives. It doesn't even make logical sense; what good is a carry-on to a dead person? But under pressure, their most deeply held values surfaced.

It's easier to handle possessions and money without loving them when we realize that we don't truly own them. Everything ultimately belongs to God.

Author Greg Laurie shares the story of a woman who had finished shopping and headed to the parking lot to return to her car. To her shock, she found four men sitting in the car. She dropped her shopping bags, drew a handgun, and screamed, "I have a gun, and I will use it! Get out of the car!" The men immediately scrambled out of the car.

The woman, somewhat shaken, loaded her shopping bags, and then got into the car. But no matter how she tried, she could not get her key into the ignition. Then it dawned on her: it was not her car. She realized that her identical model was several spaces away! She found her car and drove herself to the police station to turn herself in. The desk sergeant nearly fell out of his chair laughing. He pointed to the other counter where four men were reporting a carjacking by an old woman who had curly white hair, was less than five feet tall, and was wearing thick glasses and carrying a large handgun. No charges were filed.

The woman acted badly because she thought the car was hers when it actually belonged to someone else.

It is easy to think our money and possessions belong to us. But, actually, everything we have ultimately belongs to God. (Did you ever see a hearse pulling a U-Haul trailer?) We are just temporarily handling the money and possessions we have, "for we brought nothing into the world, and we can take nothing out of it" (1 Tim. 6:7).

Like the old woman, we will act badly if we think possessions belong to us.

One of the best ways to ensure that our relationship with money is healthy is to give some away. First Timothy 6:18 instructs us to be generous: "Command them to do good, to be rich in good deeds, and to be generous and willing to share." If we do not obey God's command to give generously, then money has become a rival god. We are obeying money's commands instead of the Lord's.

Think of the most generous person you know. Do you like that person? I suspect the answer is yes, because generosity is attractive. Generous people develop an expansive spirit that makes others enjoy their presence. Generous people both receive and give joy.

Another key to living peacefully with money is learning to be content with what we have. First Timothy 6:6 says, "But godliness with contentment is great gain." No matter how wealthy they are, if you ask people how much money they need to be content, most of them will answer, "A little more." It is not wrong to have financial goals, but make sure generosity is one of those goals.

A spiritual seeker checked into a monastery for a personal retreat. "I hope your stay is a blessed one," said the monk who showed the visitor to his cell. "If you need anything, let us know, and we'll teach you how to live without it."[14]

---

14. Philip Yancey, "For God's Sake," *Christianity Today*, March 1, 2006, https://www.christianitytoday.com/ct/2006/march/21.112.html.

▶ Prayer

Jesus, show me where my true values are. Protect my heart from the allure of money and help me be generous. Amen.

Scripture reading — write verse
  underline impt

Observe
Apply
Prayer

Day 28

Working It Out

For Individual Reflection

1. **Give thanks to God** for his faithfulness, goodness, and activity in your life.

2. **Pray** Psalm 139:23–24:

   Search me, God, and know my heart;
   *   test me and know my anxious thoughts.*
   See if there is any offensive way in me,
   *   and lead me in the way everlasting.*

   Pause and open yourself to anything the Holy Spirit might bring to your attention.

3. **Review your week.**
   a. How did I act on what God told me last week?
   b. Where have I noticed God at work?

4. **Respond.**
    a. What stood out the most from this week's readings? Where is God asking me to focus my attention this week?
    b. What will I do in response?

Group Discussion Questions

1. Do you like to blend in or stand out? How has this influenced your spiritual life?

2. In what ways has Jesus changed your thinking? What pattern of thinking would you like to ask God to change?

3. Share a time you have paid a price for following Jesus. What was that like? Is there something God is calling you to do now that will carry a price?

4. Why is it impossible to be Jesus' disciple unless we die to ourselves?

5. Why does viewing pornography damage our spiritual growth? Why is it important to tell a fellow believer about your struggle in order to get free?

6. "Money is a rival god." Agree or disagree? Why?

Week 5

The Justice of Jesus

He has shown you, O mortal, what
is good.
    And what does the LORD require
    of you?
To act justly and to love mercy
    and to walk humbly with your God.
                            —Micah 6:8

Here is my servant whom I have
    chosen,
    the one I love, in whom I delight;
I will put my Spirit on him,
    and he will proclaim justice to
    the nations.

                            —Matthew 12:18

"Doing justice" meant not only "not
doing wrong," but also actively
doing right and restoring what is
broken.

                        —Jessica Nicholas

Day 29

Just, Like Jesus

▶ **Read Matthew 12:15–21.**

When my son was a teenager, he collected model trains. He was especially interested in locomotives of a specific size and gauge. One day, he was browsing on eBay and saw an engine that he had been hunting. It was not cheap; the seller was asking for hundreds of dollars. But my son had a job, and he wanted that engine. He contacted the seller and made the purchase. Then he waited anxiously for the train to come. And he waited. And he waited. The train never arrived.

My son tried contacting the seller, but he got no response. An unscrupulous merchant had lied and stolen from my son, who was never able to recover his money. As a father, that made my blood boil. I can still feel the indignation as I write this. What kind of a person would do such a thing? How could they live with themselves? This shady character was getting away with a crime against my son, and I couldn't stand it. I wanted justice.

Something inside each of us revolts against injustice and demands fairness. It grates on us to see wrong prevail. That innate desire for justice is an echo of God's character. Humans reflect the image of God, and the Scriptures reveal that God is just.

The Old Testament prophets proclaimed that God cared more about how people treated each other than he did about their religious practices. For example:

> Stop bringing meaningless offerings!
>> Your incense is detestable to me.
> New Moons, Sabbaths and convocations—
>> I cannot bear your worthless assemblies.
> Your New Moon feasts and your appointed
>> festivals
>> I hate with all my being.
> They have become a burden to me;
>> I am weary of bearing them.
> When you spread out your hands in prayer,
>> I hide my eyes from you;
> even when you offer many prayers,
>> I am not listening.
>
> Your hands are full of blood!
>
> Wash and make yourselves clean.
>> Take your evil deeds out of my sight;
>> stop doing wrong.
> Learn to do right; seek justice.
>> Defend the oppressed.
> Take up the cause of the fatherless;
>> plead the case of the widow. (Isa. 1:13–17)

The Lord could not be clearer: he takes no pleasure in our worship and prayer if we are ignoring his laws and acting unjustly. God wants those who are oppressing widows (or teenage boys) to repent before they come to him in worship.

The New Testament points out that Jesus fulfilled the prophecies that the Messiah would express God's passion for justice:

> Here is my servant whom I have chosen,
>> the one I love, in whom I delight;
> I will put my Spirit on him,
>> and *he will proclaim justice* to the nations.
> He will not quarrel or cry out;
>> no one will hear his voice in the streets.
> A bruised reed he will not break,
>> and a smoldering wick he will not snuff out,
> till *he has brought justice* through to victory.
>> (Matt. 12:18–20, emphasis added)

God cares deeply about justice and Jesus modeled that. Part of growing in the image of Jesus is caring about justice like he does. Jesus taught us to love our neighbors as ourselves, and that means being fair and just with them.

History records that Christians have led the charge to change some of society's greatest ills.

For example, Christians were instrumental in the early movement to abolish slavery in the Western world. The British antislavery movement was led by William Wilberforce, who came to Christ while in his twenties. Motivated and guided by his faith, Wilberforce worked tirelessly to abolish the slave trade and to outlaw slavery in all overseas British territories. He was influenced by John Newton, who was a slave trader until he came to Christ. Newton became a pastor and wrote the timeless lyrics, "Amazing grace, how sweet the sound, that saved a wretch like me."

Christians also led the efforts to abolish slavery in the United States. Starting around 1830, Christians began organizing to change the laws of the land. Their faith convinced them that God created all people equal and that everyone should be treated with dignity.

Acting on their conviction carried a price, though. In the years leading up to the Civil War, Christian abolitionists became the most hated men and women in America. In the southern states, rewards were offered for killing them. In the northern states, they were shouted down in meetings, beaten, and abused. Their houses were burned down. For the thirty years leading up to the Civil War, the word *abolitionist* was an insult.[1] However, driven by their faith, they pressed on until all slaves were freed.

Christ-followers also played an essential role in the fall of Communism in Eastern Europe. The Catholic church (and its Polish pope) was hugely influential in the birth of the Polish pro-democracy Solidarity movement. Adrian Pabst writes that without Christianity, the Cold War would not have ended peacefully.[2]

Today, believers are attacking contemporary ills like human trafficking, extreme poverty, addiction, and other human brokenness.

God's concern for justice prompts some believers to organize in order to help those in need. Others express

---

1. Tim Stafford, "The Abolitionists," *Christianity Today*, https://www.christianitytoday.com/history/issues/issue-33/abolitionists.html.
2. Adrian Pabst, "Christianity Ended the Cold War Peacefully," *The Guardian*, November 11, 2009, https://www.theguardian.com/commentisfree/belief/2009/nov/10/religion-christianity.

that concern in more individual ways around their neighborhood and workplaces. We cannot overcome all of the world's ills, but that should not keep us from making all the difference we can.

▶ Prayer

Jesus, help me to care about justice as you do. Amen.

Day 30

Kingdom Greatness

▶ **Read Philippians 2:5–11.**

A forty-year-old white man in jeans, a long-sleeved T-shirt, and a Washington Nationals baseball cap found a spot next to a garbage can near the entrance of the Washington metro station. He pulled a violin from a small case and placed the open case at his feet. As most buskers do, he threw in a few dollars as seed money and began to play.

He spent the next forty-three minutes playing immortal classics by Mozart and Schubert as a parade of people streamed by. This violinist was no ordinary street musician, however, and he didn't need the money. His name is Joshua Bell, and he is one of the finest concert violinists in the world. The violin he was playing was a Stradivarius made in 1713 and worth over $3.5 million.

The *Washington Post* newspaper had arranged for him to play at the metro as an experiment in whether people would recognize greatness and beauty in unlikely places. That day, 1,097 people passed by Bell's concert.

Seven people stopped to listen to him play. Only one person recognized him.

That same week, Bell played to capacity concert hall crowds paying at least $100 per ticket. At the subway, Bell collected a total of about $32 from the twenty-seven people who stopped long enough to donate.[3]

It is understandable that most people did not recognize Bell. Even if they were classical music buffs, no one expects to come upon a world-renowned virtuoso playing in the subway.

No one expected that God would appear on earth in the form of a servant either. Yet Philippians 2:5–7 tells us that is exactly what happened:

> In your relationships with one another, have the
>   same mindset as Christ Jesus:
> Who, being in very nature God,
>   did not consider equality with God
>   something to be used to his own
>   advantage;
> rather, he made himself nothing
>   by taking the very nature of a servant,
>   being made in human likeness.

Jesus did not come to earth claiming his rights and privilege as God. Instead, he came as a servant. He lived in obedience to God and for the benefit of others. And Philippians 2:5 says we are to be servants too.

Many aspire to be leaders; fewer seek to become servants. Upward mobility is more appealing than

---

3. Gene Weingarten, "Pearls before Breakfast," *Washington Post*, April 8, 2007.

descending to servant status. Yet living a Jesus-shaped life means taking on a servant's mindset.

To grow in servanthood, be open for any assignment.

Years ago, a commercial for a shipping company showed an employee training a new hire. She explained that from time to time, he would be required to send packages, but with the new shipping system, it was easy.

The new hire responded, "I'm sorry; I don't do shipping."

The trainer looked surprised. The newbie explained in a superior tone, "I have an MBA."

"Oh, you have an MBA," the trainer replied, "then I'll have to show you how to do it."

When someone acts like they are too important to perform a particular task, it doesn't remind us of Jesus, does it? Jesus is the Son of God. Through him all things were made (Col. 1:16). And yet, he did not pick and choose which ways he would serve. He simply obeyed his heavenly Father.

To grow in servanthood, serve without expectation.

Servants don't seek the limelight. They usually work behind the scenes. They do not expect payback. Rick Warren said that the real test of whether we are a servant is how we react when someone treats us like one.

To grow in servanthood, serve unnoticed.

One winter day, a driver was waiting his turn at the toll booth when he saw a driver in an adjacent line jump out and run to the car ahead of him. He quickly brushed the snow off the car's roof and back windshield, then hopped back into his own car without saying a word. It was a random act of road kindness.

It is easy to let our attitudes slip from "service" to "serve us." To prevent that from happening, try meeting a need without anyone discovering that you were the one who did it. Stay alert to spot needs around your house, neighborhood, or workplace. Then pick a need and meet it. Enjoy blessing people in secret. Who knows, the idea might even catch on with others, and you will have started a chain reaction of blessing!

In Luke 22:27b Jesus said, "But I am among you as one who serves." When we are being shaped into Jesus' image, the same will be said about us.

▶ Prayer

Lord, keep me alert to the needs of others, and help me to know which needs to meet. Amen.

Day 31

Love Made Visible

▶ **Read James 2:14–26.**

Stephen Foster and Peggy got married in 1973, and they decided to spend their honeymoon in Angola. At the time, they did not realize that they would spend their lives in that nation, raising their four children and providing medical care for those who had none.

Foster grew up in Zaire as the son of missionary parents. After he completed his medical training in Toronto, he moved to Angola, where a bloody civil war was raging. The ruling Marxist regime was hostile to Christians, but he was able to obtain a visa because the country desperately needed doctors. (More than half of Angola's residents still have no access to health care.)

Publicly, the Marxist government officials told him they were going to make all churches disappear within twenty years. Privately, however, they admitted, "You are the only ones we know willing to serve in the midst of the fire."[4]

---

4. Nicholas Kristof, "A Little Respect for Dr. Foster," *New York Times*, March 28, 2015.

Dr. Foster helped establish a medical center in Lubango, where he performs more than a thousand surgeries each year.

"Retirement isn't in our vocabulary," said his wife, Peggy, when she was sixty-five years old. "We need more people involved. We are always encouraging people to step outside what they know, come and see what they can do. There are so many different ways they can help."[5]

What motivated the Fosters to spend their lives serving the medical needs of Angola? Angola is not an easy place to live and serve. Eleven of Foster's colleagues have been killed while ministering there. Why not just open a medical practice in Canada or the United States where life is more comfortable and the money more plentiful?

The Fosters will tell you that it is their faith in Jesus Christ that motivates and sustains them. They are followers of Jesus, who taught us to love God and to love our neighbors as ourselves (Matt. 22:37–39). Love is more than a warm feeling; when we love people, we serve them and meet their needs. They will be able to tell that we love them by watching what we do.

James 2:14–17 asks us:

What good is it, my brothers and sisters, if someone claims to have faith but has no deeds? Can such faith save them? Suppose a brother or a sister is without clothes and daily food. If one of you says to them, "Go in peace; keep warm and well fed," but does nothing about their physical

5. "Missionary Surgeon Dedicates His Life to Improving Health Care in Angola," *Red Deer Advocate*, April 5, 2014.

needs, what good is it? In the same way, faith by itself, if it is not accompanied by action, is dead.

The Fosters' faith is alive. They saw that most Angolans had no medical care available to them. They could not walk away saying, "Be warm and stay healthy," knowing they have the training and capacity to help. The Fosters love God and love people, so they could not worship God while people died of easily preventable illnesses.

Serving is love made visible. When we love someone, we do what we can to meet their needs. If your children had not eaten in two days, you would spare no effort in finding them food as quickly as you could. Your love for them would not allow you to rest while they remained hungry. When we are Jesus-shaped, we show love for God and people.

Meeting the needs of others also helps advance the gospel.

Because the Fosters have demonstrated their compassion and care for the Angolan people, they have earned the right to be heard when they speak about God's love. People listen when they say, "God loves you," because they can see that the Fosters love them.

Some people will not be able to hear that God loves them until they experience our love. An increasing number of Americans say they do not belong to any faith. Many do not even have friends who are followers of Jesus. God is not on their radar. Meeting needs in Jesus' name can build a bridge between God's kingdom and unreached people.

We all admire the Fosters' work, but we do not need to move to Africa to serve others. There are plenty of needs within a stone's throw of you right now. Your family members have needs. Can you name some? Your colleagues at work have needs; are you aware of any? If we ask God to help us notice the needs of others, he will. He can give us such an awareness of needs that we get into a habit of spotting them.

We can also financially support ministries that are meeting needs in other parts of the world. For example, you can support children in need through ministries like Compassion International. It is a blessing to know you are helping children grow both physically and spiritually.

If you are ready to take another step in your spiritual journey, consider going on a mission trip. Many believers who go on short-term mission trips come back spiritually and emotionally revitalized. That is because there is something energizing about participating in God's purposes and showing love to people in practical ways.

Anyone can complain about the state of the world today. It's easy to point out problems. However, Jesus doesn't command us to criticize the world; he calls us to change it.

▶ Prayer

Lord, let me see the needs around me and be ready to meet them by your love. Amen.

Day 32

Bridging the Racial Divide

▶ **Read John 4:1–26.**

More than fifty years ago, Rev. Martin Luther King Jr. noted: "It is appalling that the most segregated hour of Christian America is eleven o'clock on Sunday morning."[6]

Sadly, five decades later, churches are still segregated by race. Today, in any major American city, one can find white churches, African American churches, Asian churches, Latino churches, and any number of other ethnic churches. Precious few are truly multiethnic.

It may be human nature to gather with those most like ourselves, but it does not reflect God's nature. Since God is the Creator of all people, and all races will spend eternity together with him, why can't we live in community here on earth?

Jesus demonstrated the kingdom of God by not letting racial barriers keep him from connecting with others.

---

6. "Meet the Press," NBC News, April 17, 1960, https://www .youtube.com/watch?v=1q881g1L_d8.

For example, in Jesus' day, most Jews considered Samaritans unclean and inferior. There were strict laws that kept Jews from associating with Samaritans. Yet, in John 4:7–10 we read that Jesus reached out to help a Samaritan woman find new life:

> When a Samaritan woman came to draw water, Jesus said to her, "Will you give me a drink?" (His disciples had gone into the town to buy food.)
>
> The Samaritan woman said to him, "You are a Jew and I am a Samaritan woman. How can you ask me for a drink?" (For Jews do not associate with Samaritans.)
>
> Jesus answered her, "If you knew the gift of God and who it is that asks you for a drink, you would have asked him and he would have given you living water."

Jesus pointed the woman to the Father, and her life changed. If he had followed the era's custom of ethnic separation, that woman would have missed knowing God. Racial barriers advance Satan's aims and prevent God's will from being done.

The Lord first announced to Abraham that he was choosing his descendants (the Jews) to become his people. In Genesis 12:2–3 God says:

> I will make you into a great nation,
>   and I will bless you;
> I will make your name great,
>   and you will be a blessing. . . .
> and *all peoples on earth*
>   will be blessed through you." (emphasis
>   added)

From the beginning, God intended that all nations know him and that his chosen people should bless all the peoples of the earth. And through Jesus, that is what happened.

Centuries later, God created a new people for himself: the church. When the church was born on the day of Pentecost, Acts 2:5 says, "Now there were staying in Jerusalem God-fearing Jews *from every nation under heaven*" (emphasis added).

Pentecost was an annual Jewish feast. It drew people from around the world. Many of those pilgrims heard the gospel and became followers of Jesus on Pentecost. That means that from its first day, the church of Jesus was multiethnic and multinational.

Finally, in the book of Revelation, we see a glimpse of heaven, where God's will is completely fulfilled. Again, it is global:

> After this I looked, and there before me was a great multitude that no one could count, *from every nation, tribe, people and language,* standing before the throne and before the Lamb. They were wearing white robes and were holding palm branches in their hands. (Rev. 7:9, emphasis added)

From Genesis to Revelation, we see God creating a people comprised of all nations and races. He intends for his people to live together in unity.

Multiethnic churches not only model God's intent, they also seem to release his power in a special way. For example, the Azusa Street revival in the early 1900s started in a poor African American section of Los Angeles and ended up changing the course of Christian history around the world.

When those revival meetings began, blacks, whites, Latinos, and Asians, young and old, came together to experience the power of the Holy Spirit. Miracles and salvations transformed people in profound ways. Today more than 600 million people around the world claim Pentecostal heritage, and it is the fastest-growing segment of the global church.

The Azusa meetings lasted continually for nine years before they finally ended. Many believe that the revival ended because of interpersonal and racial conflict. When divisions start, revival stops.

Ephesians 4:3 says, "Make every effort to keep the unity of the Spirit through the bond of peace." We are all one in Jesus, regardless of race.

I once heard Bill Hybels challenge believers to be honest about where they stood in their attitude toward people of different races. He outlined four categories and asked us to consider which one best described us.

The first type is the *active racist*. If this is you, you tell the jokes and use the slurs that devalue people. You fear and maybe hate people of other races. If this is you, you don't have to stay that way! First John 4:20 says that if we say we love God and yet hate people, we are liars. The Bible says to repent: change your mind about what is right in God's sight. Ask the Holy Spirit, and he will give you love for others.

A second type is the *passive racist*. If this describes you, then you don't tell the jokes or use the hurtful words, but you don't stop others from doing so. You don't do anything to oppose the problem of racism. Martin Luther King Jr.

said, "In the end, we will remember not the words of our enemies but the silence of our friends."[7]

A third type is the *beginning reconciler*. You have begun to recognize that there is a problem, and you want to do something about it. You realize that people of other races have different experiences than you. You understand that the playing field has not been level for four hundred years, since slavery.

Finally, there is the *advocate* for racial reconciliation. You have decided that you are going to love indiscriminately and that you are going to look for every opportunity to bridge the divide. You are going to be active in helping God's will be done on earth as it is in heaven.

Which of these four types best describes you? What direction are you moving—toward God's purpose of reconciliation or away from it?

▶ Prayer

Lord, show me how to be a reconciler and reflect your kingdom. Amen.

---

7. Martin Luther King Jr., *The Trumpet of Conscience*, Steeler Lecture, Nov. 1967.

Day 33

Jesus in Disguise

▶ **Read Matthew 25:31–46.**

Many years ago, I attended a Pittsburgh Pirates baseball game with some fellow church members. We arrived early enough to do some tailgating in the parking lot before the game. As we were enjoying our food and one another, a poorly dressed man approached us. He said he was homeless and asked if we could give him some money. My mind instantly went to the guidance I had heard: "If you give money to a beggar, they will use it to buy drugs or alcohol." So, I replied, "Sorry, we can't give you money, but I happen to know that there is a homeless shelter nearby. They will be glad to help you out."

The man walked away, and my sense of peace left with him. I felt convicted that I had not acted in a way that pleased God and had set a poor example for the church members who were with me. My failure was not just that I should have given the man money; I could have invited the man to eat with us and asked him about his story. What God wanted from me was to see the man as valuable and show him respect. I had treated that man as a problem to solve, but God sees the poor very differently.

In Matthew 25, Jesus teaches his disciples to recognize the value of the poor. He actually said that our eternal destinies are tied to the way we treat the poor.

> Then the King will say to those on his right, "Come, you who are blessed by my Father; take your inheritance, the kingdom prepared for you since the creation of the world. For I was hungry and you gave me something to eat, I was thirsty and you gave me something to drink, I was a stranger and you invited me in, I needed clothes and you clothed me, I was sick and you looked after me, I was in prison and you came to visit me." (vv. 34–36)

In the verses that follow, the people express surprise that God is rewarding them and inviting them into eternal life. They had no idea that God took such notice of their simple acts of charity. Little did they realize that giving a scruffy guy a sandwich and a drink would register in heaven. They had no idea God took it personally.

> Then the righteous will answer him, "Lord, when did we see you hungry and feed you, or thirsty and give you something to drink? When did we see you a stranger and invite you in, or needing clothes and clothe you? When did we see you sick or in prison and go to visit you?"
>
> The King will reply, "Truly I tell you, whatever you did for one of the least of these brothers and sisters of mine, you did for me." (vv. 37–40)

We might wonder: *Aren't we saved by grace and not by feeding the poor?* Yes, we are saved by grace through faith, not by our good works (Eph. 2:8–9). However, the book of James makes it clear that the kind of faith that saves is a faith that motivates action. Caring about the poor is a sign that the love of God is transforming our hearts.

The message of Matthew 25 could not be more explicit: the way we treat the poor is the way we treat Jesus.

The Scriptures reveal that the poor are God's favorite people. Here are just a few examples:

When Jesus began his public ministry, he announced his mission with words from the Old Testament: "The Spirit of the Lord is on me, because he has anointed me to proclaim good news to the poor" (Luke 4:18).

In the Sermon on the Mount, Jesus told his listeners: "Blessed are you who are poor, for yours is the kingdom of God" (Luke 6:20).

When a wealthy young man asked Jesus about how to grow spiritually, Jesus said, "Go, sell your possessions and give to the poor, and you will have treasure in heaven. Then come, follow me" (Matt. 19:21).

After a dishonest tax collector met Jesus, everyone knew God had changed his heart because he publicly said to Jesus, "Look, Lord! Here and now I give half of my possessions to the poor, and if I have cheated anybody out of anything, I will pay back four times the amount" (Luke 19:8).

Part of growing into the image of Jesus means viewing the poor as he does. That starts with seeing them and noticing them.

Imagine that no one ever looked at you. How would that make you feel? Most people look down to avoid eye contact with homeless people when they pass them on the street. What if the next time you see a homeless person, you make eye contact? It is a simple way to communicate human dignity.

Recently, our small group created care packages for homeless people. We went shopping and then stuffed plastic bags with practical supplies that would be helpful for someone living on the streets. I put a few in my car to have them at the ready. Pulling up to a stoplight in my hometown, I saw a man holding a sign asking for help. I discovered that he had been there often, but I had never noticed him before! I waved him over to my car and gave him the bag. He looked at it and said, "All right! God bless you!" And God did.

▶ Prayer

Jesus, help me see you in the poor around me today. Amen.

Day 34

Good Works and Good News

▶ Read Luke 9:1–17.

On December 26, 2004, the Indian Ocean unexpectedly and swiftly pulled away from the Indonesian coastline, exposing the seafloor. After an eerie silence, the sea roared toward land in a 100-foot-high wall. In a matter of minutes, the explosive force of the tsunami killed more than 225,000 people in fourteen countries. The provincial capital of Banda Aceh was devastated. Most of the town's buildings and infrastructure were wiped out, and loss of life was massive.

Thousands of miles away, Pastor Jimmy Seibert and the people of Antioch Church in Waco, Texas, learned of the disaster through the news. Within hours, they were mobilizing teams to go assist in the emergency response. The church quickly raised more than $200,000, and their first team of volunteers arrived in Banda Aceh within a week, bringing hope in Jesus' name.

Each team was determined to do whatever was needed to serve the people and show them Christ. Where there were orphans, they took them in. They bound up the wounded. They met practical needs in the name of Jesus. The teams provided food, played games with children, and prayed for the injured, especially where there was no medicine available.

Over the next year, Antioch Church raised more than $1.3 million to reconstruct an entire fishing village. Locals and mission teams worked side by side to build what was dubbed "Restoration Village." A long-term mission team stayed behind to equip the people to begin a church-planting movement in the region. Through the love and witness of Antioch members, many locals came to faith in Jesus.

However, not everyone approved of Antioch's evangelistic efforts. Articles criticizing the church's work began to appear both in Hindu and American news outlets, with titles like "Mix of Quake Aid and Preaching Stirs Concern."[8] Other Christian groups opposed Antioch's mixing of faith with their meeting of practical needs.

Lead pastor Jimmy Seibert was asked for comment and said:

> When you love Jesus, you share who you are. You never make anyone convert by giving him or her aid and expecting something in return. We give everything freely, but we cannot *not* share who we are. We cannot *not* share the message

---

8. David Rohde, "Mix of Quake Aid and Preaching Stirs Concern," *New York Times*, January 22, 2005, https://www.nytimes.com/2005/01/22/world/worldspecial4/mix-of-quake-aid-and-preaching-stirs-concern.html.

of eternal life. If another tsunami had come weeks later and we had not shared the message of eternal life found in Jesus Christ, more people would have died and lived in a Christ-less eternity. It is a have-to to share the gospel . . . it is who we are.[9]

Pastor Seibert was emphasizing that it is impossible to follow Jesus without both showing God's love and sharing his message. The two are inseparable.

Jesus demonstrated his love both by meeting practical needs and by proclaiming the message of God's kingdom. He preached and healed. And he equipped his followers to do the same thing. Luke 9 records the first time Jesus sent his followers out on a short-term mission. Verse 2 says, "He sent them out to proclaim the kingdom of God and to heal the sick." Jesus taught his followers to do just what he did: heal and preach.

First John 3:8 says, "The reason the Son of God appeared was to destroy the devil's work." The devil works to harm people spiritually, physically, and relationally. Healing and preaching restore people to the physical and spiritual wholeness God originally intended.

When we work for social justice, we advance the kingdom of God. That is, God's will is "done, on earth as it is in heaven" (Matt. 6:10). That is why we work to dismantle racial discrimination and exploitation: to express God's love and thwart Satan's aims.

John Wesley led thousands to faith in Christ through his preaching. He and his team helped spark a revival

9. Jimmy Seibert, *The Church Can Change the World: Living from the Inside Out* (Waco, TX: Antioch Community Church, 2008), 227.

movement that transformed both England and the United States. Even as he preached the gospel, he also worked for prison reform, education, clean water, and housing. He even wrote a book on diet and exercise called *Primitive Physick* to help keep the early Methodists healthy! Wesley's faith in Jesus led him to heal and to preach. He embraced both social holiness and personal godliness because he loved people.

When we embrace a Jesus-shaped life, we will be committed to both the good news and the good works of Jesus. Even though the two are connected, they are not equal in priority.

I recently read a newspaper article that featured a local church serving Thanksgiving dinner to hundreds of people in their neighborhood. I was pleased to see an area church recognized for such positive and important ministry. At the same time, I knew that the newspaper would never write an article about a church proclaiming the gospel to hundreds of people. Social justice is in vogue today, but proclaiming the gospel is not. The culture will approve of the church feeding bodies but not souls.

Christ-followers are to love their neighbors in practical ways. (In fact, our church also provided hundreds of Thanksgiving dinners to people.) If we proclaim the gospel without caring for those in need, our devotion is hollow. But the Lions Club can provide people with turkey dinners. Only the church can offer the gospel that changes someone's eternity.

If we get so busy doing good works that we neglect proclaiming the good news, we touch people's physical lives while leaving them spiritually lost. Conversely, if we only proclaim the gospel while ignoring their practical needs, people will not listen to us or understand God's love for them.

Good works and good news are both essential, but the good news is the most vital because the gospel is "the power of God that brings salvation to everyone who believes" (Rom. 1:16).

▶ Prayer

Lord, show me how to both do your good works and share your good news. Amen.

Day 35

Working It Out

1. **Give thanks to God** for his faithfulness, goodness, and activity in your life.

2. **Pray** Psalm 139:23–24:

   Search me, God, and know my heart;
   *   test me and know my anxious thoughts.*
   See if there is any offensive way in me,
   *   and lead me in the way everlasting.*

Pause and open yourself to anything the Holy Spirit might bring to your attention.

3. **Review your week.**
   a. How did I act on what God told me last week?
   b. Where have I noticed God at work?

4. **Respond.**
   a. What stood out the most from this week's readings? Where is God asking me to focus my attention this week?
   b. What will I do in response?

Group Discussion Questions

1. What injustice or need in the world stirs you most? In prayer, ask God how he feels about this issue and what he wants you to do in response.

2. Which of the following aspects of being a servant is easiest for you? Which is the hardest?
   • Serve any need
   • Serve without expectation of return
   • Serve unnoticed

3. Share a time you felt loved or cared about because someone met a need you had.

4. Which of Hybels's four categories describe your participation in the racial divide?
   a. Active racist
   b. Passive racist
   c. Beginning reconciler
   d. Advocate

5. In Matthew 25 Jesus said, "Truly I tell you, whatever you did for one of the least of these brothers and sisters of mine, you did for me" (v. 40). How have you cared for the least of these?

6. Why are good works and good deeds inseparable in expanding God's kingdom?

Week 6

The Mission of Jesus

"For the Son of Man came to seek and to save the lost."

—Luke 19:10

"Therefore go and make disciples of all nations, baptizing them in the name of the Father and of the Son and of the Holy Spirit, and teaching them to obey everything I have commanded you. And surely I am with you always, to the very end of the age."

—Matthew 28:19–20

The Church exists for nothing else but to draw men into Christ, to make them little Christs. If they are not doing that, all the cathedrals, clergy, missions, sermons, even the Bible itself, are simply a waste of time. God became Man for no other purpose.

—C. S. Lewis

Day 36

Sharing Jesus' Purpose

▶ **Read Luke 15.**

When I was a college student, I shared a house with several other Christian guys. One night, one of my housemates burst through the front door, pumping his fist in the air. He exclaimed that he had just led a fellow student to Christ. His excitement was contagious.

My housemate's joy over influencing a friend toward Jesus made a lasting impression on me. It helped me realize that sharing the gospel is not just a part of following Jesus, it is central to growing in his image.

If we want to become like Jesus, then the question becomes: What is Jesus like? The previous chapters highlighted various aspects of his character. In these final days, we will look at how Jesus' nature naturally leads him to his mission.

In Luke 15, Jesus tells three parables. Their plots are similar: a shepherd leaves the ninety-nine sheep in his flock to search for one who strayed; a woman loses a valuable coin and overturns her house to find it; and a father waits and watches for his rebellious son to return home.

Each of these stories carries the same theme: something of value is lost, and there is rejoicing when it is found. By telling three parables that convey the same message, Jesus is driving home a key point: people are precious to God. Even when they rebel or wander far from him, he doesn't forget about them or write them off. Instead, he goes out of his way to search for them. Jesus is the image of God (Col. 1:15), so we would expect that he would share that same priority. And he does. Jesus stated that his mission is "to seek and to save the lost" (Luke 19:10).

If we are going to follow Jesus, we need to go where he is going, which is to the lost. It is impossible to take on Jesus' character and remain disinterested in his mission. The reverse is also true: we cannot accomplish his mission without sharing in his character.

R. York Moore wrote a book titled *Growing Your Faith by Giving It Away*. It is a memorable way of saying that as we pursue Jesus' mission to seek and to save the lost, we become more like him. There are several reasons why this is true.

Sharing the gospel motivates us to live like Jesus.

When we plan to share our faith with people, it influences the way we act around them. If you just screamed at your neighbor for letting his dog fertilize your lawn, it is not the best time to tell him about how Jesus changed your life. Or, if you are going to tell your coworkers that Jesus loves them, then it is not wise to gossip about them over lunch.

I went to get my hair cut recently. When I arrived for my appointment, I was told that my stylist would be with me in just a moment. However, she wasn't. She had double-booked my hour, and it took another half-hour before I was shown to the chair.

I hate to admit it, but I felt annoyed as I walked toward her station. I don't like taking time out of my day to get a haircut in the first place; I made the appointment so that I wouldn't have to wait. I had arrived on time, but I still wasted a half hour.

As I greeted the stylist, I lectured myself: "Steve, she probably knows that you are a pastor, so just be patient and chill out." The last thing I wanted to do was to reflect badly on Jesus by indulging in some self-centered irritability. I knew that if I ever wanted to tell her about the hope we have in Jesus, I needed to be understanding. So, I asked the Holy Spirit to help me, and he did! Choosing to ignore my impatience and lean on God's strength allowed me to tell her, "No problem," about the wait and mean it.

I don't tell you that story to pat myself on the back. I'm painfully aware that I do not yet reflect Jesus 100 percent of the time. My point is that if I had not been aware of representing Jesus, I would have been less forgiving and more irritated. Looking for opportunities to share the gospel prompts us to live like people are watching.

When we share our faith, we grasp it more fully ourselves.

One of the best ways to learn is to teach. In order to explain a subject, we need to understand it. For example, teaching algebra requires we understand how to solve equations thoroughly enough to explain it to someone else.

First Peter 3:15 tells us: "Always be prepared to give an answer to everyone who asks you to give the reason for the hope that you have." When we tell someone else about our faith, it forces us to think through questions we might otherwise ignore. Why does everyone need Jesus? What did Jesus do for us that we can't do for ourselves? Explaining the gospel to others deepens our own conviction.

When we share our faith, we must depend on the Holy Spirit.

Jesus commissioned his followers to go into the whole world and make disciples (Matt. 28:19). But first, he told them, wait for the Holy Spirit (Luke 24:49; Acts 1:4–5). They could not win the world to Christ without the power of the Holy Spirit because it takes the Spirit of God to do the mission of God.

When we are looking for openings to share the good news, we will be listening for the whisper of the Holy Spirit. He will help us know whom we should talk with and how to approach the subject. Developing a habit of leaning on God's guidance helps us become like Jesus as well as share his message.

▶ **For the next several days, let's pray this same simple prayer:**

Lord, I ask you to give me your love and urgency for those who are far from you. Amen.

$\mathcal{D}ay$ 37

Urgency

▶ **Read Luke 19:41–44.**

At 11:40 p.m. on April 14, 1912, the *Titanic* struck an iceberg off the coast of Newfoundland and began taking on water. As a precautionary move, passengers were loaded into lifeboats, which were then lowered into the water. When precaution became emergency, Fifth Officer Harold Lowe boarded Lifeboat 14 and assumed command.

Under Lowe's orders, Lifeboat 14 was lowered away from the *Titanic* at 1:25 a.m. They were 150 yards away from the ship when it sank forever beneath the icy water.

Although his lifeboat was filled, Lowe quickly realized that there were hundreds of other passengers floating in the freezing water. Although most of the other twenty lifeboats were less than half full, none rowed toward the cries of the drowning. Instead, they kept their distance for fear that desperate people would rush their boats and capsize them.

Lowe responded differently. He decided to transfer all the passengers from Lifeboat 14 into the other lifeboats. Then his boat made the 150-yard journey back to the wreck site. Amidst the countless floating dead, they found a few passengers who were still alive.

After rescuing all they could find, Lowe noticed Lifeboat D was drifting aimlessly. They threw a rope to it and towed it to the *Carpathia*, which was standing by to rescue all who could reach it.

As they were rowing toward the *Carpathia*, Lowe's crew spotted another boat (Lifeboat A) that appeared to be sinking. Making a beeline for the vessel, they discovered thirteen survivors clinging to it. Lifeboat 14 rescued them all.

Lowe and the crew of Lifeboat 14 found themselves in an emergency and did something about it. People were dying. Lowe's team had the ability to save some of them, so they did. Although they could not rescue everyone, they did what they could and made a difference.

As followers of Christ, we, too, face an emergency. Every day, we live and work with people who are spiritually dead. They are in grave danger because they have not received new life from Jesus.

However, few of us live with a sense of urgency about this crisis. Many of our coworkers, friends, and family are genuinely likable people. It is hard to think of them as being in eternal danger. The very thought can be disturbing. It is much easier to ignore it.

If we do not allow ourselves to be disturbed, we will develop no urgency. And without urgency, we will not take action.

Humanitarian agencies know that we need to see the need before we respond. If we simply hear that every ten seconds a child dies because of hunger-related causes, we might think, *That's too bad*, and immediately return to what we were doing. However, if we see a picture of a starving child, that can get our attention. Further, if we were in that nation and held some dying children and felt how light their bodies were and looked into their blank eyes, that would grab our hearts. If we held a starving child as she took her last breath, we might be undone.

The clearer we can see the brutal realities of a person who is unconnected to God, the more our urgency will grow.

Urgency grows when we see the reality of a wasted life.

Each of us is trading our lives for something. We fill our days and spend our time on what matters most to us.

If you have a growing relationship with Jesus, whatever you do has eternal significance, regardless of whether it is considered important now.

However, friends who are living apart from Christ are trading their lives for nothing. For them, everything is temporary—holding no ultimate purpose or meaning. Nothing matters because it is all lost in the end. No matter what their job or income level may be, in eternity it will be irrelevant. Without Jesus, even our important relationships will not extend past this life. No one can fulfill God's purpose for their lives if they do not know the God who made them.

When we realize that our unreached neighbors and friends will have nothing at the end of their lives, it can produce a sense of urgency in us.

Urgency grows when we see the reality of facing a crisis without God.

At some point, everyone faces a crisis. It might be a job loss, a marriage blown apart, a betrayal, an alarming medical diagnosis, or some other trauma.

When we know Jesus, we have a power beyond ourselves to meet those crises. God said he will never leave or forsake us (Deut. 31:6; Heb. 13:5). But without a growing relationship with Jesus, we will face those challenges with only human power.

When my sons were still preschoolers, I remember wondering what the world would be like when they were raising children. Looking at the trends, I was not confident that it would be a better place. I was concerned for them until I realized that, although I could not shield them from the challenges of life, I could lead them toward Jesus. Then, no matter what happened, the Lord would be present to guide and empower them. They would be all right. That motivated me to lead them toward their own relationship with Christ.

Urgency grows when we see the reality of eternity without God.

One of the passengers on the *Titanic* was evangelist John Harper. When the alarm sounded, he saw that his six-year-old daughter was safely aboard a lifeboat, then he ran through the ship talking with people about their readiness for eternity. Eventually, he had to leap into the water. As he clung to some debris, he asked another man: "Are you saved?" The man answered: "No." John replied:

"Believe on the Lord Jesus Christ and you will be saved." Shortly thereafter, they both slipped under the water.[1]

John Harper had an urgency about sharing the gospel because the reality of eternity was vividly clear in that moment.

Jesus promised that those who follow him will live with him even after their bodies die. He said we have eternal life, and he rose from the dead to back it up.

But the Bible also says that without a growing relationship with Jesus, we don't have eternal life—only death.

Every person you see today, tomorrow, this week, is in one of two conditions: either they know Jesus and have eternal life, or they do not.

John Knox was a leader of the Reformation in Scotland in the sixteenth century. It's recorded that he prayed for his country with intense passion. He cried, "O Lord, give me Scotland, or I die."[2] God gave him Scotland.

▶ Prayer

Lord, I ask you to give me your love and urgency for those who are far from you. Amen.

---

1. Dan Graves, "While the Titanic Sank, John Harper Preached," Christianity.com, May 3, 2010, https://www.christianity.com /church/church-history/timeline/1901-2000/while-titanic-sank -john-harper-preached-11630699.html.
2. Brian G. Najapfour, "'Give Me Scotland or I Die': John Knox as a Man of Prayer," Biblical Spirituality Press blog, October 22, 2019. See https://biblicalspiritualitypress.org/2019/10/22/give -me-scotland-or-i-die-john-knox-as-a-man-of-prayer/.

Day 38

Glow in the Dark

▶ **Read Matthew 5:13–16.**

"I don't have the gift."

"I need to focus on my own spiritual growth right now."

"I don't know enough about the Bible."

These are all common explanations Christians give for not sharing their faith. Maybe you could add several more.

However, I believe one of the primary reasons believers do not share their faith is that they simply do not know how. Subconsciously, we might assume it is complicated, scary, time-consuming, or unnatural to talk about Jesus. But it is not.

There is a simple way to communicate Jesus to the people where you live, work, and play. If you are a follower of Jesus, you can do it. You don't need to get an advanced theological degree. It won't require you to attend a ten-week training program. You don't need to learn a new language or technique. It is not complicated. You do not need to add an extra night a week to pull it off. You can do it in the course of your normal day.

Are you curious about how to help people experience Jesus? Bless them.

BLESS is an acronym representing a simple, five-step strategy that can help you influence people around you toward Jesus:

Begin with prayer.

Listen.

Eat with people.

Serve them.

Story (tell your story and God's story).

That's it. That's how you can help people around you encounter Jesus.

Okay, I'll give you a little more than the phrase. Here is an overview of what it looks like to take each of those steps.

Begin with prayer.

Before we talk to people about God, we talk to God about people. To be an influence for Jesus where you work begins simply: pray for your coworkers. To influence your neighbors, pray for them.

Ask for God to reveal himself to them. Pray that they have a hunger to know God. Pray for any needs you know they have. They won't know that you are doing it, but it will make a difference.

When we pray repeatedly for others, we start to care more deeply about them. It creates a bond between us. Praying for people also can soften their hearts, opening them up to the Holy Spirit's work. That's why we begin with prayer; it makes all the other steps more effective.

What if you prayed by name each day for the people who live on your street?[3] What might God do if you prayed for the members of your softball team or those you exercise with?

Listen and eat together.

These are simple ways to get to know other people. For some of us introverts, forming new relationships can be intimidating. However, these two steps are manageable and natural.

Invite a coworker to lunch. Something good happens when we eat together. Then ask questions and listen. Ask them what they like to do on weekends or about their favorite movies. When you find something they are interested in, invite them to say more. Later, you can ask more about their past experiences or hopes. This will build a relational bridge.

I was on an airplane seated next to a young woman who had her foot in a cast. She told me that she was a lawyer from Brazil traveling with her husband. I asked her about what happened to her foot, and she told me she had come to the United States for an operation that would have been risky in Brazil.

I inquired about her job, and she told me that she had started her own law practice. She went on to describe some of the challenges she faced as a lawyer in Brazil.

---

3. A great tool for praying for your neighborhood is BlessEveryHome.com. This site provides the names of those living around you and sends a daily prayer prompt with several names. It also shows the number of people praying in your area.

Eventually, she asked me what I did. I usually try to avoid answering that question as long as I can because it is not unusual for people to get quiet when I tell them I am a pastor. But when I told her, she was bold in her response. She started offering me her opinions about the church and spirituality.

I told her that what I liked best about being a pastor is seeing lives change by the power of God. Then she became quiet and reflective. She confessed: "I don't think I'm making a difference in the world. That's what is really important, isn't it?"

I answered that I believe God gave her a lot of gifts and that she could make a difference where she was. She replied that she was going to start doing something about that when she got home.

A lot can happen when we build a bridge by asking questions.

Serve others.

Notice one of their needs and meet it. There is no better way to demonstrate that we care than to meet a person's need.

To discover where people need help, all we need do is observe and listen. Ask the Lord to make you aware of other people's needs. He will be faithful to answer that prayer.

Share your story.

When we get to know people, at some point, it will be natural to talk about spiritual things. If we stay alert, there will be a moment when it will be natural to share what a difference Jesus has made in our lives.

Think through your three-minute faith story. What was your life like before Christ? How did you start a growing relationship with Jesus? What has your life been like since following Christ? Answer each of these questions in one minute, and you have a way to share your faith whenever the opportunity arises.

Go ahead, bless the people you live, work, and play with![4]

▶ Prayer

Lord, I ask you to give me your love and urgency for those who are far from you. Amen.

---

4. A helpful resource is Dave and Jon Ferguson's book *B.L.E.S.S.: 5 Everyday Ways to Love Your Neighbor and Change the World* (Washington D.C.: Salem Books, 2021).

$\mathcal{D}ay$ 39

Use Your Words

▶ Read Matthew 28:1–10.

Even though I am a preacher, I still do not like to be mocked for talking about Jesus. But, sometimes, I risk it.

A couple of years ago, our church's pastoral team was attending a seminar in Florida. One afternoon, the session was held on the campus of a large university. Without warning us, the leader instructed us to find a partner and fan out across campus to start a conversation with someone about Jesus. They said, "You've got an hour. Go."

As we walked along the tree-lined paths of the campus, I was not enjoying the scenery. Instead, I was nervous. For one thing, I'm no longer college-aged. I wondered how students would react when a random old guy approached them and started talking about Jesus. I did not imagine a pleasant encounter.

So, I asked God to point someone out to me. I waited, but didn't receive an impression about anyone in particular. After about thirty minutes, I decided that the next person I saw standing still would be the one I'd talk with.

Moments later, we came across a young man who was standing outside of a dorm.

"Hey—do you have a minute?" I asked. He did, and I asked his opinion about a survey question that was designed to start a spiritual conversation. From the answer he gave, it was apparent that he had never been to a church, let alone decided to follow Christ. He said he had never looked for God in his life. I told him that God was looking for him and that God loved him.

Our conversation lasted less than five minutes. I would like to say that the guy dropped to his knees and confessed Christ, but that is not what happened. However, I believe that the Lord used that conversation to bring him a step closer to Jesus. I trust that the next time someone talks to him about Jesus, it will make even more sense to him. I walked away exhilarated by the opportunity to speak with an unreached person about Jesus. All it took was pushing myself outside my comfort zone and speaking up.

Why take the risk and go through the effort of speaking up about Jesus?

Romans 1:16 says, "For I am not ashamed of the gospel, because it is the power of God that brings salvation to everyone who believes: first to the Jew, then to the Gentile."

The unreached people in our neighborhoods, work-places, and families will not put their faith in Christ without hearing the message of the good news. It is our privilege and responsibility to share it with them.

It might be more comfortable to avoid the risk of talking with others about Jesus. We could tell ourselves: *I'll just live a good life, and that will be my witness.* After all, hasn't it been said that we should "preach the gospel at all times" and only "use words if necessary"?[5]

The reality is, words are always necessary. The word *gospel* means "good news." Have you ever seen a news report with no words? I haven't. Effective news reports have pictures that illustrate the report. The testimony of our lives is hugely important. It is to be an illustration of the power of God. For example, we can't tell people about Jesus' love while we are acting in a selfish, hateful manner.

However, if we want people to know and follow Christ, we need to speak the message of the news as well. Otherwise, people will simply think we're just naturally good people. Without hearing the message, they will have no way to know that God is calling them to repent of their sin, trust Christ, and ask him for a new life. They won't know that salvation is a free gift, not something we earn (Eph. 2:8–9). The only way they will know is if we tell them.

On the morning Jesus rose from the dead, some women went to the tomb to finish Jesus' burial procedure. They were surprised to find an empty tomb. As they were wondering about this, an angel appeared.

> The angel said to the women, "Do not be afraid, for I know that you are looking for Jesus, who was crucified. He is not here; he has risen, just as he said. Come and see the place where he lay. Then go quickly and tell his disciples: 'He has risen from the dead and is going ahead of you into Galilee. There you will see him.' Now I have told you."

---

5. This quote has been misattributed to Saint Francis of Assisi.

So the women hurried away from the tomb, afraid yet filled with joy, and ran to tell his disciples. Suddenly Jesus met them. "Greetings," he said. They came to him, clasped his feet and worshiped him. Then Jesus said to them, "Do not be afraid. Go and tell my brothers to go to Galilee; there they will see me." (Matt. 28:5–10)

Notice that both the angel and the Lord instruct the women to go tell the other disciples that Jesus is alive. What if the women did not go on to do that? What if they rationalized, "We don't need to use words to tell others that Jesus is alive. We are just going to live good lives and that will be enough." The idea is too crazy to think about. Jesus is alive! That is astounding, earth-shaking news. They had to proclaim it. And they did. They ran to tell the other disciples.

When it comes to the gospel, our heavenly Father is telling us the same thing earthly parents say to their children: "Use your words."

▶ Prayer

Lord, I ask you to give me your love and urgency for those who are far from you. Amen.

Day 40

Working It Out

For Individual Reflection

1. **Give thanks to God** for his faithfulness, goodness, and activity in your life.

2. **Pray** Psalm 139:23–24:

    Search me, God, and know my heart;
    *   test me and know my anxious thoughts.*
    See if there is any offensive way in me,
    *   and lead me in the way everlasting.*

Pause and open yourself to anything the Holy Spirit might bring to your attention.

3. **Review your week.**
    a. How did I act on what God told me last week?
    b. Where have I noticed God at work?

4. **Respond.**

   a. What stood out the most from this week's readings? Where is God asking me to focus my attention this week?

   b. What will I do in response?

Group Discussion Questions

1. Sharing the faith/evangelism is an essential part of being a follower of Jesus. Do you agree or disagree? Why?

2. On a scale of 1 to 10, what level of urgency do you feel about the spiritually lost around you? Why?

3. What does the acronym BLESS stand for? What step would God have you take toward blessing someone this week?

4. Share your three-minute testimony:
   - Your life before Christ
   - How you began a growing relationship with Christ
   - Your life since you have been following Christ

Printed in the USA
CPSIA information can be obtained
at www.ICGtesting.com
LVHW020224260124
769364LV00003B/6